The Relationships Between Job Characteristics, Job Satisfaction, and Turnover Intention Among Software Developers

by

Timothy Lee Doré

ISBN: 1-58112-270-5

DISSERTATION.COM

Boca Raton, Florida
USA • 2005

The Relationships Between Job Characteristics, Job Satisfaction, and Turnover Intention Among Software Developers

Dissertation.com
Boca Raton, Florida
USA • 2005

ISBN: 1-58112-270-5

THE RELATIONSHIPS BETWEEN JOB CHARACTERISTICS, JOB SATISFACTION, AND

TURNOVER INTENTION AMONG SOFTWARE DEVELOPERS

A Dissertation

Presented to the
Faculty of Argosy University-Orange County

In Partial Fulfillment of
The Requirements for the Degree of

Doctor of Business Administration

by

Timothy Lee Doré

July 2004

Abstract of Dissertation Presented to the
Graduate School of Argosy University-Orange County
in Partial Fulfillment of the Requirements for the
Degree of Doctor of Business Administration

THE RELATIONSHIPS BETWEEN JOB CHARACTERISTICS, JOB SATISFACTION, AND
TURNOVER INTENTION AMONG SOFTWARE DEVELOPERS

by

Timothy Lee Doré

2004

Chairperson: Dr. Judith L. Forbes
Committee: Dr. Caryl Culp
               Dr. Paul Bramhall

Department: School of Business

Software developer turnover can have disastrous effects on an organization due to the

loss of business process knowledge, as well as acquired technical skills. Annual rates of turnover

in information technology (IT) departments have been estimated at 20% or more with the cost of

replacing technology workers ranging from 1.5 to 2.5 times annual salaries. This study purposely

focused only on software developers as opposed to IT employees in general due to the critical

nature of their work.

The factors leading to turnover intention in this field are poorly understood; therefore,

this study was designed to further understand the relationships between job characteristics, job

satisfaction, and turnover intention among software developers. 326 web surveys were

completed that contained questions relating to job characteristics, job satisfaction, turnover

intention, and demographic information. The first four job characteristics are specific to software developers while the last five job characteristics and the job satisfaction scales are from the Hackman and Oldham Job Diagnostic Survey (JDS).

Two research questions, sixteen hypotheses, and a theoretical path model were developed to understand which job characteristic variables contribute to the various dimensions of job satisfaction and which job satisfaction dimensions contribute to turnover intention. Additionally, the indirect effects of job characteristics through job satisfaction on turnover intention were also determined. The statistical testing consisted of descriptive and inferential statistical analysis. Bivariate correlations are presented, as well as path analysis, an extension of multiple regression analysis.

The results of the study uncovered several factors that can influence turnover intention among software developers. Identified in the study as statistically significant job characteristics that can be influenced by management are training, autonomy, feedback, number of developers, task significance, and skill variety. With the results of this study, management can better understand the unique needs of software developers and design development jobs to ensure that these needs are met. The study concludes with implications for practitioners and recommendations for future research.

THE RELATIONSHIPS BETWEEN JOB CHARACTERISTICS, JOB SATISFACTION, AND

TURNOVER INTENTION AMONG SOFTWARE DEVELOPERS

A Dissertation

Presented to the
Faculty of Argosy University-Orange County

In Partial Fulfillment of
The Requirements for the Degree of

Doctor of Business Administration

By

Timothy Lee Doré

July 2004

THE RELATIONSHIPS BETWEEN JOB CHARACTERISTICS, JOB SATISFACTION, AND

TURNOVER INTENTION AMONG SOFTWARE DEVELOPERS

A Dissertation

Presented to the
Faculty of Argosy University-Orange County
In Partial Fulfillment of
The Requirements for the Degree of
Doctor of Business Administration

by

Timothy Lee Doré

Argosy University-Orange County

Orange, California

July 2004

Dissertation Committee Approval:

Judith L. Forbes, Ph.D. Chairperson	11/29/14 Date
Caryl Culp, Ph.D. Member	Ray William London, Ph.D., LL.M. Program Chair, Graduate Programs
Paul Bramhall, Ph.D. Member	Joseph M. Vo, Ind./Org. PsyD Dean, School of Business

DEDICATION

I dedicate this dissertation to Susie, the center of my universe, my best friend, lover, wife, confidant, mother, and camping buddy. Without you, I never would have realized my potential.

ACKNOWLEDGEMENTS

My sincerest thanks go to my committee members, Dr. Judie Forbes, Dr. Paul Bramhall, and Dr. Caryl Culp. Extra special thanks again to Dr. Judie Forbes, my Dissertation Chairperson, for her support, guidance, patience, and encouragement. She has been a great mentor and cheerleader, and without her gentle prodding I would probably still be working on this thing!

I would also like to acknowledge the support I have received from all of my family members, and in particular my wife Susie and my younger children David and Lesley for giving me the time and freedom to work on my dissertation, when it would have been a lot more fun to hang with Dad. Thanks also to Grandma Keith, my older kids Paul and Scott, step-kids Robin, David, and Tricia, and all the grandkids, Kyle, Kelsey, Jacob, Sarah, and Matthew for giving me the time and space while I spent the past 6 years earning my Masters and Doctorate. Your love, support, and understanding has made all this possible.

I would like to thank my grandparents Nana and Gandhi and my in-laws Nick and Katie Loogman for teaching me to always strive to be better, and to never quit learning. They are no longer with us, but still remain a huge influence in my life.

I would also like to thank Mark Wysong, CEO and co-founder of Dolphin Software in Lake Oswego, Oregon for giving me the time and financial resources to pursue my education. Mark and Dolphin are one of a kind, and Dolphin is a place that I wish everyone could experience.

Lastly, I thank God for making me who I am, and giving me the brains, determination, and guts to complete this journey, and for bringing Susie into my life.

TABLE OF CONTENTS

LIST OF TABLES

CHAPTER ONE: THE PROBLEM

Software developers are charged with the task of knowing a user's job in such a thorough manner that they can design, code, and implement a computerized system to perform some or all of the user's tasks. To be successful, a software developer must attain an intimate knowledge of all aspects of the business, as well as the technical skills to make computerization a successful reality. Software developer turnover can have disastrous effects on an organization due to the loss of business process knowledge along with acquired technical skills. A review of the literature shows that the factors leading to turnover intention in this field are poorly understood; therefore, this dissertation seeks to understand the relationships between job characteristics, job satisfaction, and turnover intention among software developers

Problem Background

According to data from the Current Population Survey (CPS; a joint effort of the United States Departments of Labor and Commerce), the number of "computer systems analysts and scientists" (including programmers and engineers) increased by 190% between 1983 and 1998, more than six times faster than the 30.4% growth rate of U.S. jobs overall (Meares & Sargent, 1999). The annual job growth rate was especially marked for computer systems analysts and scientists as opposed to programmers. Even after the unexpected "dot.com bust" that ravaged technology industries and the overall downturn of the U.S. economy, the demand for core IT professionals remains high and is expected to rise over the coming years.

Not unexpectedly, an offshoot of the soaring demands for information technology (IT) professionals has been high turnover. Annual rates of turnover in IT departments have been estimated at up to 20% or more (S. Alexander, 1998; S.M. Alexander, 1999; Cone, 1998; Fryer, 1998; Kosseff, 1999; Shurn-Hannah, 2000; Thatcher, Stepna, & Boyle, 2002-03). The only exception to this trend is in research and development (R&D), which includes software designers, research scientists, engineers, and project and product managers. Turnover for R&D professionals ranges from a high of 9.2% in the computer and electronics sector to a low of 3.6% in general manufacturing, rates that are well below the national average of 15% for all U.S. industry (Kochanski & Ledford, 2001).

The general consensus across industries and organizations is that the loss of skilled IT professionals is expensive. Estimates of the cost of replacing technology workers range from roughly 1.5 times their annual salaries (Kosseff, 1999) to 2.5 times annual salaries (Longenecker & Scazzero, 2003). For R&D professionals, estimates range from one to seven times the employee's salary (Kochanski & Ledford, 2001). In addition to the cost of replacing experienced IT staff, turnover takes its toll on productivity and morale though disruptions of projects, heavier workloads, and negative impact on team cohesion. Industry experts propose that the cost of losing a scientist or engineer can be three to six times the cost of losing a manager (Kochanski & Ledford, 2001).

Some sources view high turnover as an inevitable consequence of the tremendous demand for technology skills. From this perspective, rational models of turnover, which assume job dissatisfaction is the first step toward leaving, are insufficient for explaining turnover among IT professionals (Rouse, 2001). Rouse argues that "Due to the incredible demand for qualified IT

2

professionals, unsolicited job offers are constantly bombarding members of this group." Thus, "Even though there is nothing dissatisfying about their current position, the new offer may be too good to forego" (p. 285). Utilizing a comprehensive model that takes economic factors into account, Thatcher et al. (2002-03) concluded that while job market opportunities have a definite impact on the intentions of IT workers to quit, this effect can be offset by organizational programs that provide IT employees with more rewards. In fact, many companies have successfully reduced turnover by creating a work environment that provides IT professionals with the challenging and creative work, professional status and recognition, advancement opportunities, and technology training that are routinely identified as key factors in recruiting and retaining skilled software developers.

Literature Review

The present study holds the rationale that turnover intentions among software developers are largely in agreement with theoretical models of job satisfaction, organizational commitment, and turnover. Research on turnover and retention in IT does not so much support the claim that IT turnover can be independent of job dissatisfaction, but rather suggests that "IT employees seem to be quicker to change jobs than other employees when they are dissatisfied with their current employer" (Hacker, 2003, p. 14). The fact that organizations of varying sizes and across industry sectors have effectively reduced turnover through aggressive strategies that take into account the preferences of IT professionals clearly shows that high turnover is not an "inevitable" consequence of the technology field, but rather a problem that can be successfully addressed by understanding the root causes and adopting proven strategies such as work redesign and strategic alignment of management and IT.

3

Ironically, while industry experts are acutely aware of the expense involved in replacing skilled technology staff, the problem is exacerbated by the fact that executive management often lacks understanding of the full economic impact of high technology turnover (Kochanski & Ledford, 2001). Outside of the technology sector, IT has traditionally been excluded from strategic management operations. A major consequence of this outdated practice is that managerially oriented IT employees are deprived of opportunities for advancement while technically oriented employees are frustrated by lack of professional respect, recognition, and challenge (Hopkins, 1998). In large corporations, IT staffers often report feeling frustrated when their jobs involve maintaining systems rather than working on new projects (Goldstein, 1989; McEachern, 2001). Overall, the historical "disconnect between the business line and the IT department" (McEachern, 2001, p. 44) is a key contributor to job dissatisfaction among software developers and consequently to turnover intentions.

For software developers in high technology firms, turnover is more often related to organizational upheaval, restructuring, and instability (Baron, Hannan, & Burton, 2001; Walsh, 2001). Additionally, the business environment in the technology sector is characterized by short product life cycles, intense market competition, and pressures from clients to complete projects "on time and within budget" (Meares & Sargent, 1999, p. 9). Unrelenting pressures and sometimes unrealistic expectations and deadlines can make IT professionals especially vulnerable to work exhaustion and burnout (Moore, 2000). This problem is not limited to software developers employed in technology companies; in fact, job pressures may be perceived more negatively by programmers whose jobs entail maintenance and who thus lack the challenge and innovation of working with cutting edge technologies. By definition, "IT workers are

4

expected to keep technologies working and computer applications functioning around the clock in organizations" (Moore, 2000, p. 144). Excessive demands on time (including ubiquitous reports of being on call on weekends and vacations) can easily lead to work exhaustion. Studies within and outside of the IT field consistently find correlations between work exhaustion and intentions to leave.

In addition to job dissatisfaction and burnout, which transcend professional boundaries as causes of voluntary turnover, other job features are unique to IT occupations. First, as Rouse (2001) observed, IT employees are more likely to be approached by recruiters than most other professional groups. A 1999 *InformationWeek* survey disclosed that more than two-thirds of IT professionals had been contacted by a headhunter within a year; in fact, they received an average of three prospects in six months (Meares & Sargent, 1999). The percentage was only slightly lower in the 2000 survey: 60% of IT staff and 67% of IT managers reported being approached by headhunters with the same average frequency (Zurier, 2000). The competition is particularly powerful for employees with "hot skills," such as Java or data mining experience (Meares & Sargent, 1999).

Second, the rapid obsolescence of acquired knowledge and skills that characterizes IT has contributed to a "mindset" in which changing jobs frequently is viewed as a professional asset as opposed to a stigma or liability (Hacker, 2003). A report by the Office of Technology Policy (OTP) stated succinctly, "Unlike so many occupations in which job stability is a hallmark of success, the business environment in IT has created a labor market in which job hopping serves as a means to gain the vital skills needed for career opportunities" (Meares & Sargent, 1999, p. 13). For many IT professionals, "Jobs are now regarded as another element of the training

5

process, of learning by doing, and employees move from job to job to gain new skill sets and experiences….Acquiring new skills allows them to move within the entire IT work community for opportunities, rather than solely within a particular company" (p. 13).

Third, "Because much of IT work is project oriented, the technical employee's loyalty may be more to the project, and not necessarily to the employer" (Hacker, 2003, p. 15). The *InformationWeek* survey reported that the average job duration was four years for IT staff members and five years for IT managers. During the dot.com boom, *Digital Nation* found that the average job stay in Silicon Valley was 18 months (Meares & Sargent, 1999, p. 13).

Although it can be argued that no theoretical model effectively captures *all* dimensions of job satisfaction and turnover, research on IT professionals is generally in agreement with the existing models. For example, Guimares and Igbaria (1992) found that for information systems (IS) and information center (IC) personnel, the most powerful predictors of turnover intentions were organizational commitment, overall job satisfaction, role dynamics, and employee age and tenure. These factors are systematically reported in business literature and appear to transcend professional and organizational boundaries.

The conceptual model proposed by Thatcher et al. (2002-03) for investigating turnover in IT employees adds economic factors. According to Thatcher et al. two disparate perspectives on turnover in IT exists. The first is consistent with Rouse's (2001) theory that IT turnover is driven by a tight labor market and soaring demands for employees with high technology skills. The second perspective does not ignore the impact of market forces, but focuses on organizational features that produce job dissatisfaction such as work overload, unrealistic demands, poor advancement opportunities, and lack of respect for technical expertise.

The findings of Thatcher et al. (2002-03) supported Steer's and Mowday's model of turnover Lee and Mowday (1987) and Hackman and Oldham's (1980) Job Characteristics Model (JCM). Organizational commitment was inversely related to turnover while intent to leave predicted actual leaving. Job satisfaction and task significance both had a positive influence on organizational commitment, and task significance, task variety, and autonomy were linked with job satisfaction. Perceptions of job alternatives did show a positive impact on intentions to leave although the effect of organizational commitment remained strong. Unlike Guimares and Igbaria (1992), Thatcher et al. (2002-03) found no effect for age. Research is inconsistent on the impact of age on turnover, although some evidence exists that younger employees are most likely to have hot skills, which makes them ready targets for headhunters (Fryer, 1998; Lu, 1999). Task significance, task variety, and autonomy are invariably cited as critical factors in job satisfaction and turnover among software developers.

The OTP report divides employers of IT professionals into two categories. In the first group are those employers *"for which IT is the core business* [emphasis in original]" (Meares & Sargent, 1999, p. 9). They stand at the cutting edge of developing and distributing new technologies where they routinely contend with short product life cycles, intense market competition, and budget and time demands. The second group of employers includes those that hire IT professionals to work on the *"application of information technologies to enhance their core businesses in other fields"* (p. 9). Pressures and intensity are lower in this sector, and product life cycles are generally longer.

The dot.com crash resulted in an exodus of IT workers from high technology firms into manufacturing, financial services, retail, and other businesses in the second category (Walsh,

7

2001). Traditionally, IT workers had left jobs in these sectors due to lack of respect for their skills and poor opportunities for advancement. Recent articles suggest that IT professionals are more interested in job security than they were when jobs were plentiful, although they invariably stress the importance of the workplace environment in attracting and retaining qualified IT staff (McEachern, 2001; Russo, 2002; Walsh, 2001; Zetlin, 2001; Zurier, 2001).

Numerous sources emphasize that even with generous financial rewards, programmers and software developers are likely to be dissatisfied in a work environment that stifles creativity and fails to respect their professional expertise; indeed, this complaint is ever present in the professional literature (Fisher, 2000; Rouse, 2001; Thatcher et al., 2002; Walsh). Conversely, firms that have effectively reduced IT turnover have generally been proactive in creating flexible working conditions and an environment that fosters innovation, challenge, and "fun" (S.M. Alexander, 1999; Cone, 1998; Zemke, 2000; Zetlin, 2001; Zurier, 2000). Investing in professional development and training as well as providing ample opportunities for IT staff to utilize new skills rank high on the list of effective retention strategies (Cone, 1998; Deakin, 2002; DeMers, 2002; Russo, 2002; Zetlin, 2001).

Two decades ago, Goldstein and Rockart (1984) attributed aspects of job dissatisfaction among programmers and analysts to the practice of focusing on technical skills to the exclusion of training and experience in management processes. To address this problem they advocated training IT employees in management skills to reduce conflict and enhance job satisfaction and productivity. Despite massive workplace upheavals, and the predominance of IT in all areas of business and industry, these recommendations have been largely ignored. In fact, the exclusion of IT staff from management training is a prominent cause of turnover. The traditional

8

dichotomy between management and IT has generated poor understanding on both sides: IT professionals lack knowledge of management processes and are thus uncertain about their roles in strategic operations; similarly, senior executives are often unaware of the valuable contribution of IT (Hopkins, 1998). The dichotomy is underscored by the fact that most chief information officers (CIOs) are not members of top management teams, resulting in very high turnover among CIOs.

Organizations that have successfully reduced IT turnover have typically expanded their training programs to include management development for IT staff in addition to opportunities to master new technologies (Deakin, 2002; Zetlin, 2001). Both types of training can be equally important in retaining IT employees. Although it may seem obvious that offering training programs in new technologies is an excellent way to retain talented workers, many organizations fear that extensive training opportunities will prove a poor return on investment: once IT workers acquire hot skills they will seek out better opportunities (Deakin, 2002; Meares & Sargent, 1999). IT executives regard this assumption as erroneous. According to Peter Jessel, CIO and managing director at Towers Perrin, "Good training satisfies the company's and the employee's objectives." The paradox is "If people feel like they have competitive skills and could easily leave and find another job, they are less prone to do it" (Deakin, 2002, p. 30). Indeed, the companies that appear on *Computerworld s* 2001 survey of "100 Best Places to Work in IT", typically offer generous opportunities for technical and non-technical training (Zetlin, 2001).

A review of the literature suggests that much of the turnover among IT professionals outside the technology sector is due to the traditional dichotomy between strategic management and IT and consequent misperceptions on each side. In fact, ample evidence exists that suggests high turnover is often related to top management's lack of awareness of the value of IT on the company's bottom line and subsequent poor recognition of the technical and managerial expertise of the IT staff. The problem is underscored by the fact that much of the research on job satisfaction among IT professionals appears in industry journals rather than organizational literature. With increasing demand for IT professionals, it is imperative that organizations become more proactive in their efforts to retain talented IT staff. The first step in doing so is to delve into the underlying causes of turnover with the goal of developing and refining appropriate job retention strategies.

Purpose of the Study

The purpose of this study is to investigate the array of factors that influences job satisfaction and turnover intentions among software developers (defined as programmers, software engineers, programmer analysts). The study utilized a web survey in order to recruit a broad, international sample. The rationale for the study is the premise that turnover among IT professionals is influenced by intrinsic and extrinsic factors that transcend professional boundaries as well as by task-related, organizational, and economic factors that are unique to IT. The existing body of research has identified a number of factors that impact job satisfaction and turnover intentions among IT employees. This study is designed to explore the dynamic interaction of these factors, which may serve as a basis for structuring programs and policies to promote the retention of IT employees across a variety of organizations.

Research Questions

Two broad research questions were addressed in this study. Each research question was related to several specific hypotheses that are described in Chapter Three. The research questions are:

1. Which job characteristic variables contribute to the various dimensions of job satisfaction among software developers?

2. Which job satisfaction dimensions contribute to turnover intention among software developers?

Limitations/Delimitations

A limitation of this study is the potential for response bias. That is, respondents to the web survey may not provide accurate information regarding their backgrounds, job characteristics, job satisfaction, or turnover intention. Additionally, this research represents a cross-section of the measured variables. No consideration is given for changes in the labor market, changes in technology, or other factors that can affect behavior in a class of workers, such as software developers, that historically has been in high demand. That is, this study did not assess every potential variable that could affect job satisfaction or turnover intention, although the most important ones, and those that are under the control of organizational management, are included. Finally, it is possible that the survey items used to assess the relevant constructs may provide unreliable or invalid scores, although every effort was made to employ the best available measures of each construct.

The primary delimitation of the study is the potential for sampling bias. The results applied only to software developers who visit the web sites and newsgroups upon which the subject recruitment occurred. It is possible that these developers represent a non-random subset of all software developers, and to the extent that this is true, the results has limited generalizability.

Definition of Terms

The following terms are defined for the purpose of this study:

1. *IT:* Information Technology, which typically refers to hardware, software, networking and telecommunications in support of a business entity.

2. *Software developer:* a technology professional with the title of Programmer, Software Engineer, or Programmer Analyst whose primary function is to design, develop, and maintain computer programs.

3. *Turnover intention*: intent to leave one's present position in an organization within a given time period.

4. *Job satisfaction:* perception(s) that a job meets one's personal expectations; for software developers a key component is a job that provides "interesting and challenging work" (Russo, 2002).

5. *Job burnout:* an extension of work exhaustion or tedium due to "too many pressures, conflict, and demands, combined with too few rewards, acknowledgements, and successes" (Moore, 2000, p. 142).

6. *Hot skills:* cutting edge skills areas that are in high demand among employers of software developers.

7. *Outsourcing:* the practice of hiring contract workers from outside the organization to perform technology-related tasks.

8. *Employee value proposition (EVP):* the complete set of intrinsic and extrinsic rewards an organization offers employees in exchange for continued employment and committed effort (Kochanski & Ledford, 2001).

Importance of the Study

The demand for skilled software developers continues to accelerate. The enrollment of young people in technology programs has not kept up with the demand, and even in the face of layoffs and downsizing, a shortage of qualified programmers, software engineers, and analysts persists. Replacing experienced IT employees is expensive, although, paradoxically, executive management is often unaware of the economic impact and the indispensable contribution of IT to strategic operations. This study represents an extensive effort to explore the factors that contribute to job satisfaction, organizational commitment, and turnover intention among programmers, software engineers, and analysts. Despite the crucial role of IT in all aspects of business and communications, a dichotomy exists between strategic management and IT that undermines job satisfaction and exacerbates turnover among IT professionals. A study of this type can provide valuable information for the persistent, although not insoluble, problem of high turnover among technology workers in organizations.

Format of the Remaining Chapters

The next chapter, Chapter Two, presents a literature review of various turnover studies relating primarily to information systems professionals. This chapter explores theoretical models that have been applied to the study of job satisfaction and turnover intention, as well as empirical research and anecdotal reports by IT professionals and industry experts. The chapter concludes with a review of "best practices" that are currently used to effectively retain IT talent.

Chapter Three describes the research methodology, theoretical path model, web survey, and how the research was conducted in support of the goals identified in Chapter One and shown to be lacking through the review of the relevant literature in Chapter Two. This chapter also presents the hypotheses and variables that were developed to answer the research questions in addition to the data analysis techniques.

Chapter Four presents a detailed discussion of the descriptive and inferential statistical data analysis. Bivariate correlations are presented, as well as multiple regression analysis allowing for a comparison between the two results. All computer generated statistical output is included in addition to detailed data analysis for each hypothesis.

The final chapter, Chapter Five, describes the findings of the study and relates the results of each hypothesis test to previous works as outlined in the Chapter Two literature review. Next, a detailed discussion of implications for practitioners is presented, and the chapter concludes with some recommendations for further research.

CHAPTER TWO: REVIEW OF THE LITERATURE

This chapter reviews current and past literature relevant to this study. The major topics are a review of the models concerning job satisfaction and dissatisfaction as it relates to turnover, and empirical studies and anecdotal reports relating to turnover and intention to turnover.

Introduction and Background

Over the past 25 years, information technology (IT) has come to occupy an exceedingly prominent place in the global economy and its pace continues to accelerate. In the 20 years between 1977 and 1998, the IT sector of the United States economy nearly doubled (from 4.2% to 8.2%) and in the two years between 1995 and 1997 IT accounted for over one-third of the country's real economic growth (Meares & Sargent, 1999). The unprecedented development inevitably led to increasing demand for professionals with specialized technical skills.

According to data from the Current Population Survey (CPS; a combined effort of the U.S. Departments of Labor and Commerce), the number of "computer systems analysts and scientists" (including programmers and engineers) increased by 190% between 1983 and 1998, more than six times faster than the 30.4% growth rate of U.S. jobs overall (Meares & Sargent, 1999). The annual job growth rate has been most impressive for computer systems analysts and scientists compared to programmers (16.4% and 3.7% respectively for 1995-1998). During the 1990s the rapid proliferation of new technologies, the Internet explosion, and the frenzied "Y2K" preparation generated rampant salary raises in the quest to secure and retain IT talent (S. Alexander, 1998; S.M. Alexander, 1999; Ende, 1998; Lu, 1999; Rouse, 2001). Although the subsequent "dot.com bust" and overall economic downturn may have dampened salary

expectations (Radke, 2003), the demand for core IT professionals is expected to rise over the

coming years (Meares & Sargent, 1999).

Not unexpectedly, a side effect of mounting demand for IT professionals has been

increased turnover. Annual rates of turnover in IT departments have been estimated at up to 20%

or more (S. Alexander, 1998; S.M. Alexander, 1999; Cone, 1998; Fryer, 1998; Kosseff, 1999;

Shurn-Hannah, 2000; Thatcher, Stepna, & Boyle, 2002-03). Turnover is lower among

professionals in research and development (R&D), which includes software designers, research

scientists, engineers, and project and product managers. A September 2000 survey reported

figures for R&D below the national average of 15% for all U.S. industry, ranging from a high of

9.2% in the computer and electronics sector to a low of 3.6% in general manufacturing

(Kochanski & Ledford, 2001).

The general consensus across industries and organizations is the loss of skilled IT

professionals is expensive. Kevin McGrath, Vice President of Human Resources (HR) at

software and programming firm Comshare, targets the cost of replacing technology workers at

roughly 1.5 times their annual salaries (Kosseff, 1999). An IT industry survey raised estimates to

2.5 time annual salary (Longenecker & Scazzero, 2003), and in R&D estimates range from one

to seven times the employee's salary (Kochanski & Ledford (2001). In addition to the cost of

replacing experienced IT staff, turnover takes its toll on productivity and morale through

disruptions of projects, heavier workloads, and impact on team cohesion. Kochanski and Ledford

(2001) propose that the cost of losing a scientist or engineer can be three to six times the cost of losing a manager, adding that many companies are unaware of the full economic impact of losing technology staff.

Rouse (2001) argues that rational models of voluntary turnover, which assume that job dissatisfaction is the first step in a linear progression toward leaving current employment, are inadequate for explaining turnover rates among IT professionals. Rouse acknowledges that even with generous financial rewards, programmers and software developers are likely to be dissatisfied in a work environment that stifles creativity and fails to respect their professional expertise; indeed, this complaint is ever present in the professional literature (Fisher, 2000; Thatcher et al., 2002-03; Walsh, 2001). Conversely, firms that have effectively reduced IT turnover have generally been proactive in creating flexible working conditions and an environment that fosters innovation, challenge, and "fun" (S.M. Alexander, 1999; Cone, 1998; Zemke, 2000; Zetlin, 2001; Zurier, 2000). Investing in professional development and training as well as providing ample opportunities for IT staff to utilize new skills rank high on the list of effective retention strategies (Cone, 1998; Deakin, 2002; DeMers, 2002; Russo, 2002; Zetlin, 2001).

Some companies have undertaken massive efforts to reduce excessive turnover. By aligning IT with business strategy, Harrah's Entertainment reduced IT turnover from 35% to 5% in a single year and ranked second (to Home Depot) in *Computerworld s* 2001 survey of "100 Best Places to Work in IT" (Zetlin, 2001). Despite such success stories, turnover of skilled IT personnel remains a hazard for most firms. Rouse (2001) contends that even given the high premium that IT professionals place on intrinsic and extrinsic rewards, the idea that job dissatisfaction necessarily underlies the decision to leave is a "flawed assumption." Instead,

17

"Due to the incredible demand for qualified IT professionals, unsolicited job offers are constantly bombarding members of this group. Even though there is nothing dissatisfying about their current position, the new offer may be too good to forego" (Rouse, 2001, p. 285).

Support for Rouse's (2001) perspective exists. A 1999 *InformationWeek* survey disclosed that more than two-thirds of IT professionals had been contacted by a headhunter within a year; in fact, they received an average of three prospects in the previous six months (Meares & Sargent, 1999). The percentage was only slightly lower in the 2000 survey: 60% of IT staff and 67% of IT managers reported being approached by headhunters with the same average frequency (Zurier, 2000). The competition is even stronger for employees with "hot skills," such as data mining experience. In this select field, 75% of IT staff and 90% of IT managers reported being approached by recruiters in the past year (Meares & Sargent, 1999).

The problem is compounded by recognition that "What might be hot skills one day could turn cold the next day," as stated by management consultant Niels Rasmussen (S.M. Alexander, 1999, p. T2). The fall of Internet enterprises generated unforeseen layoff among IT workers. As a result, some businesses have scaled back aggressive retention tactics such as frequent salary raises and bonuses (Russo, 2002), although virtually all sources stress the importance of professional development and "quality of life" issues in retaining IT staff.

Current trends suggest that firms may be focusing their efforts on retaining IT professionals with hot skills. According to industry expert John Landrine, the IT market is flooded with programmers and software engineers who have standard certifications such as Microsoft Certified Systems Engineer (MCSE) or Microsoft Certified Professional (MCP) (Radke, 2003). The Dice Tech Skills Profile, an addendum to the 2003 report from the

Information Technology Association of America (ITAA), cites Java as the most sought after skills area, with demand growing by 27% over 2002. After Java the report lists SQL, C and C++, Oracle, and Windows NT as the most in-demand skills. Whereas most IT salaries have been level over the past year, salaries in these areas have demonstrated a "modest increase." While "demand for standard certification is extremely low," in Landrine's view, hiring managers place a premium on specialty areas, notably "security and high level Web-based management" (Radke, 2003, p. 11).

Research on turnover and retention in IT does not so much support Rouse's (2001) claim that IT turnover can be independent of job dissatisfaction, but rather suggests that "IT employees seem to be quicker to change jobs than other employees when they are dissatisfied with their current employer" (Hacker, 2003, p. 14). Overall, most findings reported in both IT trade magazines and professional journals are largely in agreement with theoretical models of job satisfaction and voluntary turnover (which will be discussed in the next section). However, the rapid obsolescence of acquired knowledge and skills is unique to IT and has contributed to a "mindset" in which changing jobs frequently is viewed as a professional asset as opposed to a stigma or liability (Hacker, 2003).

A comprehensive research report sponsored by the Office of Technology Policy (OTP) stated succinctly that "Unlike so many occupations in which job stability is a hallmark of success, the business environment in IT has created a labor market in which job hopping serves as a means to gain the vital skills needed for career opportunities" (Meares & Sargent, 1999, p. 13). In support of their findings the authors cite research by the Computing Research Association, which concluded:

Jobs are now regarded as another element of the training process, of learning by doing, and employees move from job to job to gain new skill sets and experiences rather than assume they will stay with a particular company for life. Acquiring new skills allows them to move within the entire IT work community for opportunities, rather than solely within a particular company. (Meares & Sargent, 1999, p. 13)

Another contributor to the frequent job-hopping observed in IT professionals is the fact that "Because much of IT work is project oriented, the technical employee's loyalty may be more to the project, and not necessarily to the employer" (Hacker, 2003, p. 15). The *InformationWeek* survey reported that the average job duration was four years for IT staff members and five years for IT managers. During the dot.com boom, *Digital Nation* found that the average job stay in "super hot Silicon Valley" was 18 months (Meares & Sargent, 1999, p. 13).

The OTP report divides employers of IT professionals into two categories. In the first group are those employers "*for which IT is the core business* [original emphasis]" (Meares & Sargent, 1999, p. 9). They stand at the cutting edge of developing and distributing new technologies where they routinely contend with short product life cycles, intense market competition, or pressures from clients to complete projects "on time and within budget" (p. 9). The second group of employers includes those that hire IT professionals to work on the "*application of information technologies to enhance their core businesses in other fields*" (p. 9). Pressures and intensity are lower in this sector and product life cycles are generally longer.

The dot.com crash resulted in an exodus of IT workers from high technology firms into manufacturing, financial services, retail, and other businesses in the second category. Judy Karpel, president of the technical recruiting firm Hayward Simone Associates, now has a clientele composed of 85% financial services; it had dropped to 60% during the height of the Internet boom. Says Karpel, "A lot of people coming out of dot.coms are saying, 'No more startups'" (Walsh, 2001, p. 2). Indeed, the financial sector is a major beneficiary of the radical shift in IT employment patterns (Walsh, 2001). Many IT professionals had left the financial sector due to lack of respect for their skills and poor opportunities for advancement (McEachern, 2001). For example, systems analyst Pete Kelly, who left Lehman Brothers for the excitement of Uproar, an online games company, claimed that during four years with Lehman, he was "treated like little more than a 'high-tech janitor'" (Walsh, 2001, p. 3). When Uproar's stock crashed and rapid management upheaval ensued, Kelly returned to the financial sector to work for Goldman Sachs & Co. Of his new job, Kelly says, "I have the security of a Wall Street firm, and I'm still able to work with the latest Web technologies" (p.3).

Recent articles suggest that IT professionals are more interested in job security than they had been when jobs were plentiful, although they invariably stress the importance of the workplace environment in attracting and retaining qualified IT staff (McEachern, 2001; Russo, 2002; Walsh, 2001; Zetlin, 2001; Zurier, 2000). Commenting on the growing demand for Java developers, database administrators, project managers, and Web networking specialists in companies that traditionally viewed IT professionals as support staff, Dice.com director Kent Kelderman observed that "It's like the dot.coms trained these people, and now they're moving back into the bricks-and-mortar world" (Walsh, 2001, p. 4).

Financial services firms traditionally attracted IT professionals through high status and equally high salaries and compensation. The economic downturn has had a positive impact on hiring and retention in sectors that have had difficulty in attracting and retaining qualified IT staff. The food industry, which has lagged behind other industries in the adoption of advanced technologies and has had difficulty recruiting IT workers, has taken a proactive approach to recruitment and retention, offering internship programs, professional development opportunities, and a comfortable work-life balance (Russo, 2002). Municipal governments are becoming major IT employers, competing with higher private sector salaries through generous benefits packages, educational programs, and innovative job design (DeMers, 2002; Meares & Sargent, 1999).

A review of the literature indicates that the factors underlying job turnover among IT professionals tend to differ according to the two categories of employers outlined by the OTP report (Meares & Sargent, 1999). Organizational upheaval is the major cause of turnover for IT workers in technology start-ups (Baron, Hannan, & Burton, 2001); whereas those employed in non-technology firms are more often frustrated by lack of opportunities for professional growth. The role of money appears to be uncertain. For example, *InformationWeek* published two articles in one year, the first saying that salaries had flattened and money was no longer a key motivator in IT and the second saying the reverse (Meares & Sargent, 1999). All of the studies reviewed for this dissertation are inconsistent with regards to money as a motivator.

It may be fair to say that no theoretical models have yet fully captured the multidimensional nature of job satisfaction or turnover. The rapid obsolescence of technologies and increasing demand for hot skills sets IT apart from other professional fields. At the same time, the interaction of intrinsic and extrinsic rewards and the impact of job dissatisfaction on turnover are applicable to software developers as they are to other professional groups.

Models of Job Satisfaction and Turnover

This section explores theoretical models that have been applied to the study of job satisfaction and turnover or intent to turn over. Research drawn from the technology field has been compared with more general models.

Motivation and Job Satisfaction

Herzberg's motivator-hygiene theory is one of the most widely used frameworks for examining job satisfaction. Herzberg (1968/2003) based his two-factor model of motivation on research drawn from engineers and accountants, ultimately extending his research to encompass a broad array of populations. His model is based on the assumption that the factors that elicit job satisfaction and motivation are independent from those underlying job dissatisfaction. *Motivators* or growth factors derive from uniquely human qualities: "the ability to achieve and through achievement, to experience psychological growth" (Herzberg, 1968/2003, p. 91). Motivators include: "achievement, recognition for achievement, the work itself, responsibility, and growth or advancement" (pp. 91-92). The *hygiene* or dissatisfaction-avoidance factors, which are extrinsic to the job include: "company policy and administration, supervision, inter-personal relationships, working conditions, salary, status, and security" (p. 92).

Maidani (1991) applied Herzberg's theory to a study of job satisfaction among accountants and engineers (Herzberg's original subject groups) in private and public sector organizations. Contrary to Herzberg's (1968/2003) assumption, both motivator and hygiene factors emerged as sources of job satisfaction. This is significant to this study because engineers are an integral part of R&D project teams (Kochanski & Ledford, 2001). In general, research on IT professionals supports the notion that both motivator and hygiene factors are linked with job satisfaction. In fact, Harrah's IT vice president Eileen Cassini stated that a keynote of Harrah's retention strategy is attending to "hygiene factors" in the form of "basic issues such as compensation, training opportunities, and workplace flexibility" (Zetlin, 2001, p. 40). Through a complete redesign of existing policies, Harrah's turned what had been sources of dissatisfaction into powerful motivators for retaining IT staff.

Recent theories of motivation have begun to question the alleged dichotomy between intrinsic and extrinsic rewards. Amabile (1997), whose primary focus is on creativity in organizations, proposes that, "under certain conditions, certain forms of extrinsic motivation may combine synergistically with intrinsic motivation…" (p. 45). Three factors trigger this positive synergy: "the person's initial motivational state, the type of extrinsic motivator used, and the timing of the extrinsic motivation" (p. 45). Extrinsic rewards are most often enhancing for people already involved in their work. "Synergistic intrinsic motivators" include certain forms of reward, recognition, and feedback. They tend to have the greatest value when administered at certain points of the creative process. Reward, recognition, and feedback appear prominently as strategies for retaining IT talent (Tulgan, 2000; Zemke, 2000; Zetlin, 2001).

Of particular relevance to the present study, Amabile (1997) applied her synergistic model to employees engaged in projects in a large high technology firm. The factors that emerged as predictors of high creativity correspond to those routinely cited by IT professionals as positive workplace characteristics. These include: 1) *organizational encouragement* (a culture that fosters, appreciates, and fairly rewards creativity, has mechanisms that support innovation, and has a shared vision and active flow of ideas); 2) *supervisory encouragement* (a manager who serves as a positive model, sets appropriate goals, and supports and values both the work group and individual contributions); 3) *work group supports* (a work group characterized by skills diversity, honest communication, openness to innovative ideas, constructive challenge, and mutual trust, support, and commitment); 4) *challenging work* (focusing effort on challenging

24

tasks and important projects); and 5) *freedom* (autonomy and control over one's work, although this had the smallest effect on creativity).

Conversely, *organizational impediments*, which undermine creativity, reflect the type of organizational culture that yields high IT turnover rates. This detrimental culture impedes creativity through internal politics, harsh rejection of new ideas, destructive internal competition, risk-avoidance, and excessive support for the status quo (Amabile, 1997). Surprisingly, *workload pressure* (including intensive time pressures, unrealistic productivity demands, and distractions from creative work) had minimal impact on creativity. However, pressures of this type have been targeted as sources of job dissatisfaction and turnover for IT staff (Fisher, 2000; McGee, 1996).

Work Redesign and Job Satisfaction

Hackman and Oldham's classic treatise *Work Redesign* (1980) appeared at a time when American companies were coming to terms with rampant job dissatisfaction and the realization that the traditional Industrial Age organization was inadequately designed to meet productivity demands in a competitive global marketplace. A major strength of Hackman and Oldman's Job Characteristics Model (JCM; 1975, 1980) is that it is highly adaptable for different employee groups and different organizations. It is especially apt for examining job satisfaction among professionals who are highly motivated and have strong needs for autonomy, independence, and creativity. In fact, Hackman and Oldham recognized the importance of rewards, recognition, and feedback, which motivate creativity in IT workers (Amabile, 1997). Basically, the JCM specifies that several core job dimensions, such as one's level of autonomy, the variety of skills one engages in, and the perceived broad significance of one's tasks, can be used to characterize the most important variables associated with a given job. Furthermore, the model indicates that these

25

core job characteristics are predictive of levels of job satisfaction, which itself is a multi-dimensional construct.

One of the reasons for the popularity of the JCM of Hackman and Oldham (1975, 1980) is that a reliable and valid measure of the various job characteristics and job satisfaction constructs contained within the model is available. The Job Diagnostic Survey (JDS; Hackman & Oldham, 1975) contains separate scales to assess five core job characteristics (i.e. skill variety, task identity, task significance, autonomy, and feedback) and seven ways in which an individual can be satisfied or dissatisfied with a job (i.e. intrinsic work motivation, overall job satisfaction, satisfaction with job security, satisfaction with pay, social job satisfaction, satisfaction with supervision, and job growth satisfaction). A more thorough description of the JDS is provided in Chapter Three.

Hackman and Oldham's (1980) JCM was often used in early studies of job satisfaction in computer programmers and analysts. Goldstein and Rockart (1984) combined the JCM with Kahn and colleagues' model of role perceptions to explore the job factors related to job satisfaction in a sample of 125 programmer/analysts employed by four large organizations. They found that peer and supervisor leadership qualities, as well as role perceptions, were related to job satisfaction. The connection is not surprising given that role conflict and role ambiguity are often due to poor feedback and communication. In contrast, positive supervisor support and team interaction enhances creativity and satisfaction (Amabile, 1997).

Interestingly, Goldstein and Rockart (1984) attributed the problems of role conflict and role ambiguity to the focus on technical skills among IT professionals as opposed to focusing on managerial skills such as: "planning, organizing, and controlling work—and in interpersonal skills" (p. 113). Consequently they advocated training programmers and analysts in management skills to reduce conflict and enhance job satisfaction and productivity.

Two decades later the literature clearly indicates that the recommendations of Goldstein and Rockart (1984) have been largely ignored. In fact, the exclusion of IT staff from management training is a prominent cause of turnover. The traditional dichotomy between management and IT has generated poor understanding on both sides: IT professionals lack knowledge of management processes and are thus uncertain about their roles in strategic operations; similarly, senior executives are often unaware of the valuable contribution of IT (Hopkins, 1998). The dichotomy is underscored by the fact that most chief information officers (CIOs) are not members of top management teams, resulting in very high turnover among CIOs. Organizations that have successfully reduced IT turnover have typically expanded their training programs to include management development for IT staff in addition to opportunities to master new technologies (Deakin, 2002; Zetlin, 2001).

Igbaria, Greenhaus, and Parasuraman (1991) theorized that IT professionals would exhibit either technical or managerial career orientations. The sample included 464 members of the Association for Computing Machinery (ACM) who held a variety of IT positions. Technical and managerial preferences often had an inverse correlation. Systems programmers were essentially technically or autonomy oriented. Applications programmers and software engineers had similar technical orientations although they tended to be lower in managerial or autonomy orientation than systems programmers. Not surprisingly, the highest proportion of managerially oriented subjects was found among IT managers (nearly 50%); substantial proportions of systems analysts and project leaders also displayed managerial preferences. Consultants included both technical and managerial types.

Contrary to the researchers' expectations fewer than half the participants had predominant orientations that were either technical or managerial. Despite their initial predictions, Igbaria et al. (1991) noted that the fairly high proportion of autonomy oriented subjects corresponds to other studies that found high needs for autonomy and independence among IT employees. This finding is repeated throughout other recent studies. Igbaria et al. also observed that a moderate number of participants had a lifestyle orientation. That is to say that these participants had a need to balance family, career and self-development. This orientation was most often reported by software engineers and applications programmers, and was expressed by more than 20% of female participants. The authors proposed that as more women enter IT and more men assume domestic responsibilities, the lifestyle career orientation might become more common among IT professionals. Indeed, this prediction appears to be true due to a general shift toward achieving a satisfying work-life balance, particularly among younger workers (Tulgan, 2000). Strategies designed to help employees attain a comfortable balance between personal and professional life (such as flex-time and telecommuting) are a prominent part of initiatives for reducing IT turnover (DeMers, 2002; Sanminiatelli, 2000; Zetlin, 2001).

The most significant finding reported by Igbaria et al. (1991) was the importance of matching employees' career orientations to the work environment. Not unexpectedly:

> Managerially oriented employees in technical jobs and technically oriented employees in managerial jobs displayed a number of negative work attitudes, including low satisfaction and lack of commitment to the organization. This study showed that managerially oriented employees react positively to managerial jobs because they see opportunities for advancement, money, top management respect, and power in these jobs. Similarly,

because technically oriented employees see opportunities for reputation enhancement, competent colleagues, peer respect and challenging tasks in technical jobs, they are more satisfied and committed in these positions. (Igbaria et al., 1991, p. 165)

The historical gap between management and IT can undermine job satisfaction and exacerbate turnover by limiting the advancement of managerially oriented IT employees while simultaneously depriving technically oriented employees of professional respect, recognition, and challenge (Hopkins, 1998). Indeed, this problem has been targeted as the primary cause of IT turnover in financial service organizations (McEachern, 2001). Some notable exceptions appear on *Computerworld s* list of model employers. In these innovative companies, a close alignment of IT and business operations allows employees to switch between the two areas if they choose (Zetlin, 2001).

Smits, McLean, and Tanner (1993) conducted a longitudinal study of career maturation and progression to examine the personal and professional characteristics of IT professionals. The segment of their study reviewed here, which focuses on entry-level employees, included elements of Hackman and Oldham's (1980) JCM. The authors found no gender differences in personal and professional preferences with the exception that women preferred more informal supervision. As with the trend toward lifestyle orientation, this attitude has become more prevalent among younger workers in general and may be especially pronounced in IT (Tulgan, 2000).

The type of work environment preferred by the IT respondents is consistently reported in the literature. According to Smits et al. (1993) the types of "jobs and work environments preferred by this sample of high achievers are characterized by a desire for creative and challenging work that provides a sense of accomplishment, by task variety, autonomy, and completion, and by work that provides opportunities for advancement within their chosen careers" (p. 114). Indeed, organizations that fail to provide IT staff with these qualities are invariably plagued by high turnover rates. In terms of work-related qualities, the respondents viewed themselves as "punctual, industrious, organized, and capable of providing leadership resulting in goal attainment." Among their personal strengths, they perceived themselves as "intelligent, educated, insightful, and independent" (p. 114).

Amidst their personal and professional strengths, Smits et al. (1993) found one striking (although not unexpected) weakness in the personality profiles of the IT professionals: "interpersonal insensitivity, poor people skills, and a preference for working alone" (p. 114). The authors note that these traits are often "true of persons with a high learned need for achievement" (p. 114). This prominent finding reinforces the assertion of Goldstein and Rockart (1984) that IT professionals should be trained in management skills, including communication.

In their approach to managing R&D professionals, Hoyt and Gerloff (1999) drew upon prior research to divide engineers into four identified personality types:

1. *Creative* types who favor innovation and autonomy, change, risk-taking, and high-energy expenditure.

2. *Entrepreneurial* types who share many characteristics of creative types but are more socially adept.

3. *Analytic* types who are very high on complexity and order and high on organization but low on risk-taking.

4. *Development-Oriented* types who are very high on organization, high on energy and innovation, but low on risk-taking.

The categories that professionals fall into can be used to predict the roles they assume in IT and the tactics that can be used to retain them. Entrepreneurial types are most likely to leave if they feel inadequately rewarded; in fact, for those who aspire to create their own startups, it is unlikely that any rewards will be effective. Instead, they may emerge as competitors to the firms where they honed their skills. Creative types are most prone to dissatisfaction in work environments that do not provide them with stimulating, exciting work and often prefer to work alone, while analytic types are prominent among project leaders. Both creative and analytic types seek recognition and rewards for their technical expertise as well as opportunities to take on new challenges. Development-oriented types flourish in an environment of highly charged teamwork. Similar to project leaders, they are motivated by an incentive system that rewards their successes by offering them more important and challenging projects.

Hoyt and Gerloff (1999) emphasize the importance of creating a work environment that supports the orientations of all four engineering types. They note that despite the acknowledged need for innovation in the technology industry, "Unfortunately, the realities of competitive markets, budget constraints, schedules and risk of technical obsolescence often restrict freedom to be creative… These conditions ultimately produce negative motivation and stress that eventually lead to personnel turnover" (p. 289). They cite seven factors that enhance motivation for technical professionals:

1. Positive perceptions of personal status

2. Sufficient resources

3. Role clarity

4. Successful department performance

31

5. High work team morale

6. Good communications between technical and management staff

7. High levels of goal congruence

Goldstein (1989) used the JCM, role conflict, and role ambiguity to explore job satisfaction in a sample of 292 programmer/analysts working in three North American branches of a large manufacturing firm. The participants were subdivided according to the tasks they performed. Three scales categorized participants into maintenance, development, or support. Three other scales were designed to classify the developers as either programmers or analysts. Supporters were not subdivided because their tasks did not correspond to either analysis or programming, and maintainers were not subdivided due to their low representation as analysts (only 14 of 128 maintainers).

Supporters had the clearest understanding of their professional roles since they tended to be more autonomous and worked more closely with end-users (Goldstein, 1989). Overall, however, no differences surfaced in satisfaction between supporters, programmers, and analysts. Maintainers proved to be the least satisfied group, which can be attributed to lower skill variety, less feedback from users, and less certainty regarding their roles. Using Hackman and Oldham's (1980) theory, Goldstein (1989) proposed that redesigning the work of maintainers to provide them with more autonomy and more interaction with users would enhance job satisfaction.

Recent research indicates that *organizational redesign* rather than work redesign may be needed to alleviate dissatisfaction among IT employees whose work involves system maintenance. Once again this has been a prevalent problem in the financial sector, attributed to the "disconnect between the business line and the IT department" (McEachern, 2001, p. 44).

Allen Geller, managing director of A.G. Barrington has often observed this pervasive problem, taking the stance that companies should opt for strategic alignment of IT with business. Consistent with Goldstein's (1989) finding, Geller notes that in larger companies IT staff frequently feel frustrated when they are working in the "maintenance mode" instead of involved in new projects. Geller refers to maintaining systems as "babysitting."

Geller suggests outsourcing the maintenance and support tasks that core IT staffs often find tedious and consequently seek other employment to escape (McEachern, 2001). An alternative solution is to prevent tedium by "keeping initiatives small and breaking up projects," which is consistent with the tenets of work redesign. According to Larry Tabb, research director at the Tower Group, with this strategy, "there is more chance of success and the projects are completed faster so people can circulate and work on other projects in other areas" (McEachern, 2001, p. 44).

Tabb also offers advice that is in agreement with the perspectives of Igbaria et al. (1991). He suggests that companies identify what types of workers are employed in IT and deploy their skills according to their personal preferences. States Tabb, "Align people with what they want to do. If they get a kick out of new technology, get them on different projects with various new technologies, if they just want a stable position, put them in a stable role" (McEachern, 2001, p.44). Like Igbaria et al. (1991), Tabb recognizes that some IT workers prefer to achieve recognition for honing their technical skills, while others have a more managerial bent and should be encouraged in that direction (McEachern, 2001).

Dissatisfaction and Burnout

The concept of *burnout* was initially derived from research on human service professionals but has since been extended to apply to a broad range of occupations. Job burnout can be viewed as an extension of work exhaustion or tedium due to "too many pressures, conflict, and demands, combined with too few rewards, acknowledgements, and successes" (Moore, 2000, p. 142). Indeed, this definition captures the experience of many IT professionals who leave jobs in the financial sector (McEachern, 2001; Walsh, 2001).

Moore (2000) contends that certain aspects of the technology job environment can make IT professionals especially susceptible to burnout. The need to keep up with rapidly changing technologies and complete projects within (sometimes unrealistic) time and budget demands is exacerbated by the fact that "IT workers are expected to keep technologies working and computer applications functioning around the clock in organizations" (p. 144). In addition to the constant reports of being on continual beeper or on call via cell phone (often including weekends and vacation time), IT workers report being besieged by non-technology coworkers with mundane problems regarding malfunctioning office equipment (McGee, 1996; Moore, 2000).

Role conflict and role ambiguity, which undermine job satisfaction (Goldstein, 1989; Goldstein & Rockart, 1984), have been identified as contributors to burnout. Moore (2000) proposes that the boundary spanning activities that are commonplace in IT also make IT professionals vulnerable to burnout. In her study, which involved a random sample of 270 members of the Association for Information Technology Professionals (AITP), Moore included age and organizational tenure as variables that have been found to influence burnout.

Moore (2000) found that not unexpectedly, respondents scoring high on work exhaustion expressed significantly higher intentions to leave their jobs. The crucial factor appeared to be work overload. Major contributors to work overload included inadequate allotment of resources and staff and unrealistic deadlines and target dates. The most powerful predictors of turnover intention were "perceived fairness of rewards, work exhaustion, organizational tenure, and perceived workload" (p. 158). The proportion of respondents classified as exhausted was 18%, which Moore considers "a low estimate of the actual prevalence" of work exhaustion in IT (p. 150). In fact, the author emphasizes that given "the current climate of dependence on information systems and technology and high demand for IT labor," business organizations should be especially attuned to the causes of burnout and its impact on retention and turnover (p. 158).

Moore (2000) suggests that a business's "best people" in IT may be most susceptible to burnout, although no empirical evidence on this topic exists. Conversely, ample anecdotal evidence does exist that IT professionals who seek challenge and stimulation feel stifled in organizations that impede creativity and professionalism and will likely seek other employment. A letter to *Fortune* and the editor's response confirmed that programmers are burning out at a rate exceeding other workers and faster than they had been in the past. Fisher (2000) observed that this was a common phenomenon among programmers working outside of the high technology sector. Numerous letters corroborated systems analyst Kelly's complaint of being treated like a "high tech janitor" (Walsh, 2001, p. 3). Consistent with other sources, Fisher noted that this problem seems to be endemic in the financial sector (McEachern, 2001; Walsh, 2001).

Fisher (2000) cited organizational psychologist Byron Woollen, who has investigated burnout and job turnover in programmers. Woollen offered three suggestions for managers desiring to retain IT talent. First, the manager should explain not only what needs to be done but also the reason behind it. In other words, programmers should be apprised of the strategic importance of their work. The strategic alignment of IT and business is a prominent theme in enhancing productivity and retention (Hopkins, 1998; Zetlin, 2001).

The conventional separation of management and IT also underlies Woollen's second suggestion. He notes that programmers often feel "accurately" that they are denied opportunities for advancement, typically due to perceptions that their detail-orientation, analytical thinking, and tendency toward introversion preclude the ability to assume leadership positions that require good interpersonal skills. Smits et al. (1993) argue that because of these tendencies, IT professionals should be trained in business communication skills, similar to Goldstein and Rockart's (1984) recommendation that they be exposed to management skills. The relatively high proportion of managerial types in the study of Igbaria et al. (1991), combined with the dissatisfaction emanating from a poor fit between work orientation and work environment, clearly supports the need to provide IT professionals with opportunities for upward advancement. This importance is supported by industry experts (Deakin, 2002; McEachern, 2001; Russo, 2002) and confirmed by the positive impact on retention documented by companies that have eliminated the boundaries between technical and management tracks (Zetlin, 2001).

Woollen's third recommendation is a "no-brainer": ensure that IT professionals have ample opportunities to refine and develop their technical skills so they continually keep up with new technologies (Fisher, 2000). Although this would seem like an obvious way to retain talented workers, many organizations fear that offering extensive training opportunities will prove a poor return on investment: once IT workers acquire hot skills, they will seek out better opportunities (Deakin, 2002; Meares & Sargent, 1999). IT executives consider this a misguided assumption. According to Peter Jessel, CIO and managing director at Towers Perrin, "Good training satisfies the company's and the employee's objectives." The paradox is that "If people feel like they have competitive skills and could easily leave and find another job, they are less prone to do it" (Deakin, 2002, p. 30).

The companies appearing on *Computerworld s* "best places" list typically offer extensive opportunities for technical and non-technical training (Zetlin, 2001). In addition to fears of losing qualified personnel, one reason given for the relative lack of training opportunities offered IT employees is that most employers are small businesses (Meares & Sargent, 1999). However, some innovative firms do not perceive size as a barrier. A notable example is the software company Appraisal.com, which established Appraisal.com University for its 70 employees (Deakin, 2002). A year and a half after the program's inception, turnover at Appraisal.com dropped by 300% and roughly half the firm's staff attended seminars on a given day. President Mark Yellen, who calls himself the company's "chief evangelist," extols the wisdom of aligning professional development with strategic management goals: employees who fulfill personal but not company goals are fired, while those who fulfill company goals at the expense of personal goals will quit.

In essence, ongoing training effectively aligns both personal and organizational goals. Industry experts recommend benchmarking best practices as a key strategy for alleviating high turnover rates (Lu, 1999). The CIOs and IT managers interviewed by Lu invariably cited training (primarily technical training) as a critical factor in retention, in conjunction with interesting projects that offer IT workers opportunities to deploy their new skills. However, they cautioned that "Although great training opportunities and exciting projects are crucial, they are not nearly enough to keep IT staff from leaving if strong management is not in place" (Lu, 1999, p. 79). This observation has been confirmed by the high turnover that often accompanies organizational changes in high technology startups (Baron et al., 2001).

Job Satisfaction and Organizational Commitment

Research on turnover in IT offers some support for Rouse's (2001) assertion that quitting an organization is not necessarily contingent on job dissatisfaction (Hacker, 2003; Meares & Sargent, 1999). Nonetheless, both empirical and anecdotal evidence have yielded a number of factors related to job dissatisfaction that manifest in terms of high turnover rates. Vandenberg and Lance (1992) observed that despite widespread acceptance of the assumption that job satisfaction is a cause of organizational commitment, "the causal relationship between the two constructs is not clearly understood" (p. 154). To explore this issue, they surveyed 100 IT professionals employed by a multinational software R&D company. Counter to the common belief that job satisfaction is an antecedent to organizational commitment, they found the reverse to be true: organizational commitment was antecedent to job satisfaction.

Indirectly, Vandenberg and Lance's (1992) conclusion seems to support Rouse's (2001) theory. That is, IT professionals who view employment as a learning experience or short-term commitment are unlikely to feel satisfied with their jobs, especially if they perceive that they will always have new opportunities for expansion. However, although rational models of turnover may not fully explain turnover among IT employees (or perhaps any employee group), the effectiveness that concerted retention strategies have had in reducing high turnover illustrates that job satisfaction is a key factor in retaining qualified IT staff while job dissatisfaction underlies high turnover rates.

The effects of age and downsizing. Cohen (1993) conducted a meta-analysis or research on organizational commitment and turnover spanning the time frame from 1967-1991, focusing on the effects of age and organizational tenure. Based on his results, Cohen proposed that different strategies should be used to assess organizational commitment in younger or newer, and older employees. For younger employees and new hires, organizational commitment can be highly dynamic due to a variety of influences; thus, more frequent assessments are needed for more accurate predictions of intent to leave. In particular, new hires can be very enthusiastic, but easily discouraged if their initial expectations are not met. Smits et al. (1993) consider this a hazard for entry-level IT professionals who expect exciting assignments but instead are given maintenance work. They strongly recommend that new prospects are given realistic job previews that allow them to evaluate whether the job meets their expectations, or alternately, to modify their expectations accordingly. They emphasize that IT professionals are likely to be dissatisfied if the organization does not meet their needs to engage in stimulating and challenging work.

A British study of 50 graduates of an organizational graduate training program who had remained with the company for three years confirmed the importance of meeting new candidates' expectations for creative and challenging work independent of the chosen field. The 32 men and 18 women (ranging from 23-35) were unanimous in stating that salary "could never compensate for having to do a boring, un-stimulating job" (Sturges & Guest, 2001, p. 452). Being assigned tasks that were interesting and engaging fostered organizational commitment while assignment to routine or unchallenging tasks undermined it. Consistent with the literature

39

on IT professionals, opportunities for advancement had a similar effect: those who perceived opportunities for advancement were satisfied with their jobs while those who considered themselves "stuck" expressed intentions to leave. The only respects in which the graduate recruits differed from IT professionals were the relatively lower priority they gave to training and the higher premium they placed on social relationships.

For older workers, according to Cohen (1993), organizational commitment may not necessarily predict turnover because although they may be low in commitment, they may not leave due to "structural bonds, few employment opportunities, and a desire for stability" (p. 1153).

Although Cohen's (1993) assumption about older workers may have been true a decade ago, it may be less applicable today. The rampant downsizing of the late 1980s and 1990s has affected the attitudes of both younger and older workers although the mechanisms may differ. Younger employees began their careers at a time when traditional notions of job security and linear upward promotion had been demolished by radical restructuring and downsizing (Fryer, 1998; Tulgan, 2000). Many saw their parents' expectations for job security dissipate. As a result, they tend to view jobs as short-term rather than stable commitments.

Older workers may have reached similar conclusions after first-hand experiences with downsizing and lay-offs (Moses, 1997). In fact, in an unpredictable job market (exemplified by the dot.com crash), Moses advises *all* workers to think of themselves as contract workers. Interestingly, job stability ranked high on the list of preferences in *InformationWeek s* 1999 salary survey, which took place when Silicon Valley was still "super hot" (Meares & Sargent, 1999). While job instability and subsequent turnover resulting from restructuring and especially, mergers and acquisitions, is common across employment sectors, outsourcing may have a uniquely detrimental effect on perceptions of job stability among IT employees (Due, 1992; Khosrowpour & Subramanian, 1996). The effect is enhanced when outsourcing follows downsizing and lay-offs; survivors are likely to experience poor morale, heavier workloads and high stress levels, and to see their own jobs at stake. In fact, the disruption to work teams as a result of downsizing has been found to have a lingering adverse effect on creativity, even after productivity declines begin to reverse (Amabile & Conti, 1999).

Some proportion of IT workers may view changes resulting from outsourcing as opportunities for work redesign and expansion, particularly if colleagues left voluntarily instead by being laid-off (Due, 1992). In Due's observation, this effect is especially pronounced during the "honeymoon period" when the outsourcing vendor typically tries to secure the loyalty of remaining core employees through perks such as travel, training, and additional benefits.

In their survey of 146 Association for Systems Management (ASM) members, Khosrowpour & Subramanian (1996) found more support for the negative aspects of downsizing. A large majority of respondents (81%) had either negative or neutral feelings about outsourcing. Even more significant, 78% disagreed with the idea that the welfare of employees is considered in outsourcing decisions. The authors consider this finding a definite antecedent of low morale and productivity. They advocate involving employees in outsourcing decisions as a way of alleviating stress and easing the transition to the new work environment.

A recent survey by Techie.com reported that 37% of more than 1,500 employees in high technology firms had been laid off at some point in the last three years (Hacker, 2003). One-fifth

41

of respondents expressed the belief that "all jobs are temporary" (p. 16). Hacker noted a peculiar irony: "Techie.com is now out of business" (p. 16).

Most sources agree that voluntary turnover is higher among younger IT professionals. Managers have explored this problem through a variety of perspectives. The University of Michigan discovered that younger workers left in disproportionate numbers to those who had worked in IT for 10 years or more and had been promoted to management or administrative positions (Lu, 1999). They decided to examine their benefits packages to determine whether they were slanted in favor of senior employees. Work-life balance benefits tend to hold special attraction for new employees (Meares & Sargent, 1999; Russo, 2002; Tulgan, 2000).

An alternative perspective is that younger employees are most likely to have hot skills, which makes them ready targets for headhunters (Fryer, 1998; Lu, 1999). Stated by one recruiter, "Younger people with hot skills have the most options open to them. Just six to 12 months of experience can be parlayed into a significant pay increase in another job" (Fryer, 1998, p. 104).

This attitude has been expressed by representatives from organizations as diverse as Xerox and the Washington Post. As stated by Bob Monastero, HR director of Xerox's information management center, "It's the newer skilled people who cause the pressure and demand to change jobs" (Lu, 1999, p. 79). Of particular relevance to the present study, managers with both organizations perceived themselves at highest risk of losing programmer/analysts and software developers who possess cutting edge skills. At Xerox, retention strategies include several benchmark practices: a) profit-sharing, stock options, and a performance-based bonus plan; b) fully paid tuition to obtain a masters' degree or MBA at a local university; and c) options to choose between a management and technical career track to satisfy the professional development needs of IT employees with both managerial and technical orientations.

Despite threats of lay-offs and instability, few sources dispute that a shortage of skilled IT professionals exists. Ironically, the tremendous growth of new technologies has not reverberated in the career choices of young people. Enrollments in technology programs are disproportionately low, although technology graduates are most likely to be employed in their major field (Meares & Sargent, 1999). Women and minority men are particularly underrepresented in technology fields and are most often found in support functions rather than innovation and management. Due to perceived barriers to advancement, women employed in IT may have lower job satisfaction and organizational commitment than their male counterparts (Baroudi & Igbaria, 1994-95). Thatcher et al. (2002-03) found higher intentions to leave among female IT workers.

Even with the proliferation of "diversity policies," minorities in IT often feel excluded from the mainstream organizational culture, disconnected from key information channels, and under more intense scrutiny (Shurn-Hannah, 2000). In fact, some HR managers in high technology firms concede that diversity efforts are often no more than "lip service." Subtle and non-subtle forms of discrimination inevitably translate into higher turnover. Some companies are targeting retention strategies to African American and Hispanic employees; mentoring, training, and professional development opportunities, which are important for keeping all employees, may be especially critical to the retention of employees who feel themselves set apart from the core organizational culture.

Older workers who have achieved managerial or professional status may view organizational commitment as a good return on investment, as seems to have been the case with the University of Michigan IT staff (Lu, 1999). Whether senior IT professionals would choose to remain in jobs they deem unsatisfying, as suggested by Cohen's (1993) analysis, is questionable and probably dependent upon individual as well as external factors. Rather than seeing older professionals shunted aside or consigned to tedious jobs, Kochanski and Ledford (2001) predict that the impending retirement of baby boomers, combined with increasing demand for IT professionals and low enrollments in technology programs, will worsen the IT shortage and make retention even more critical.

Rational and Instinctual Models of Turnover

Steers and Mowday's model of voluntary turnover has been widely used in empirical research. According to the model, intention to stay or leave follows a clear progression: 1) job expectations ("met expectations") and values influence the person's affective responses to a job; 2) affective responses affect desire and intention to stay or leave, which in turn, is influenced by variables such as family situation; and 3) intention to leave a job is followed by actual leaving (Lee & Mowday, 1987). For some individuals, intent may directly lead to leaving, while for others it will act indirectly through the initiation of a job search and exploration of options.

Lee and Mowday (1987) tested the model on 445 employees occupying a variety of positions in a financial institution. Consistent with the model, they found that job performance, met expectations, job values, organizational characteristics, and organizational experiences influenced affective responses. Prior job performance was related to job satisfaction and organizational commitment. The only departure from their predictions was the minimal

44

interaction between intention to leave and available alternatives. The researchers note that scant evidence exists supporting a direct link between available job opportunities and quitting a job. Indeed, Rouse (2001) contends that this is precisely the weakness in applying conventional models of turnover to IT professionals.

Rouse (2001) prefers Lee and Mitchell's instinctual or "unfolding" model of turnover for predicting intention to leave among IT workers. Lee, Mitchell, Wise, and Fireman (1996) tested the model by surveying 44 nurses who had recently quit hospital jobs. In Lee and Mitchell's model, the first stage is not an appraisal but a *shock* (decision path 1). A shock is an event that starts the psychological process involved in quitting a job. For IT professionals, the "shock" frequently takes the form of an approach by a recruiter (Rouse, 2001), although it may also be upheaval in a high technology firm, or an occurrence that is not career-specific such as a spouse or partner's job offer to relocate. The shock stimulates a decision (decision path 2) in which the person evaluates the quality of his or her attachment to the organization (Lee et al., 1996). In conjunction with this evaluation, the person begins to assess the degree of attachment he or she could form with another organization (decision path 3). The two decision paths are weighed in terms of a cost-benefit analysis: if attachment to the present organization is deemed superior, the decision will be to stay; if attachment to another organization seems more attractive, the decision will be to leave (decision path 3).

Decision paths 2 and 3 trigger memories of past events that influence the evaluation of attachment to the present or prospective organizations (Lee et al., 1996). In Rouse's (2001) application of the model to IT employees, such memories may include previous unsolicited job offers that elicit comparisons with the present offer. The comparison provides sufficient

45

information for the person to decide whether or not to stay in the current job. Rouse speculates that given the relative abundance of job openings in the IT field, the decision may occur quickly with minimal fear of choosing the wrong alternative. While contending that the relative ease with which IT professionals change jobs may facilitate quick decision-making, he acknowledges that the unexpected decline of Internet ventures and the economic downturn may elicit a more comprehensive analysis of the situation before a decision is made.

The unfolding model also includes a fourth decision path in which no shock has occurred (Lee et al., 1996). In this case the decision to leave is a gradual process stemming from perceptions that the job no longer satisfies personal or professional needs, has compromised professional values, or impedes goal achievement. If dissatisfaction is especially intense, the person may quit abruptly. Alternately, dissatisfaction may lead to the exploration of alternatives consistent with Steers and Mowday or other rational models.

The survey of nurses found support for the unfolding model: "Most typically, an expected and a non-work-related shock initiated a larger sequence of decisions, behaviors, and events, in which quitting was simply a quick part of the larger process" (Lee et al., 1996, p. 28). Decision path 2 was generally initiated through a disruptive organizational event that prompted abrupt departure. Decision path 3 would be characteristic of an employee who receives an alternative job offer, and one of the subjects fit this scenario perfectly. Overall, the cases studied supported the unfolding model, although the researchers conceded that several cases revealed ambiguities in the model.

Rouse (2001) considers the unfolding model a "significant step forward" in enhancing understanding of the processes underlying voluntary job turnover. In some respects, the selection of nurses is appropriate for making comparisons to IT employees. Both groups of professionals seek professional development, respect, and recognition and both have highly sought after skills. At the same time both professional groups often feel thwarted by workplace conditions and thus dissatisfied with their jobs. Although IT workers may be more likely than other employees to leave jobs in the absence of job dissatisfaction, ample evidence exists that a sizable proportion *are* dissatisfied with their jobs. Application of the unfolding model to explore turnover in IT professionals may be a fruitful area for future research. However, Rouse acknowledges that additional research is needed to validate the model before it can be deemed an effective prediction of turnover.

Rouse (2001) recognizes that economic indicators can play a prominent role in influencing the decisions of individuals contemplating leaving their present employment. The conceptual model proposed by Thatcher et al. (2002-03) for investigating turnover in IT employees takes economic factors into account. According to Thatcher et al. two disparate perspectives exist concerning turnover in IT. The first is consistent with Rouse's (2001) theory that IT turnover is driven by a tight labor market and soaring demands for employees with high technology skills. The second perspective does not ignore the impact of market forces, but focuses instead on the organizational characteristics that produce job dissatisfaction such as work overload, unrealistic demands, poor advancement opportunities, and lack of respect for technical expertise. Thatcher et al. observed that few researchers have examined both channels simultaneously.

Participants in the study of Thatcher et al. (2002-03) included 128 men and 63 women holding a variety of IT positions in a state government. The average job tenure was high (16.26

years, although some had been employed less than a year) and average age 41.2 years. The findings supported Steer's and Mowday's model of turnover (Lee & Mowday, 1987) and Hackman and Oldham's (1980) JCM. Organizational commitment was inversely related to turnover while intent to leave predicted actual leaving. Job satisfaction and task significance both had a positive influence on organizational commitment, and task significance, task variety, and autonomy were linked with job satisfaction. Perceptions of job alternatives did show a positive impact on intentions to leave although the effect of organizational commitment remained strong. Age had no significant influence; however, women reported higher intentions to leave than did men.

Thatcher et al. (2002-03) concluded that while job market opportunities have a definite impact on the intentions of IT workers to quit, this effect can be offset by organizational programs that provide IT employees with more rewards. The extremely low turnover rates of some companies that have aggressively implemented retention strategies confirm the validity of this assumption. Thatcher et al. strongly recommend strategies that foster organizational commitment by involving employees in personal and organizational development: "Through socialization programs such as training or mentoring, organizations may cultivate and diminish the relative influence of perceived job alternatives on the turnover intention of IT workers" (p. 248). They suggest that this strategy may be particularly effective for retaining female workers. It may be especially vital for retaining minority employees (Shurn-Hannah, 2000).

Organizational commitment and socialization. King and Sethi (1998) explored the issue of socialization in terms of the role adjustment of IT professionals. Numerous studies have found that role conflict and role ambiguity are detrimental to job satisfaction (Goldstein, 1989;

48

Goldstein & Rockart, 1984; Moore, 2000). King and Sethi (1998) propose that the socialization of new hires may prevent the role conflict and role ambiguity that are endemic to IT employees. Their respondents were drawn from a cross-section of industry sectors and a wide array of IT positions; 61% of the 160 participants were engaged in systems development tasks and 31% were involved in end-user support. The average age of respondents was 27 years and organizational tenure averaged 15 months.

King and Sethi (1998) observed that individual and institutional socialization strategies acted differently on the IT workers' roles and personal adaptation to the organization. The social aspects of the socialization process, namely support and interactions from senior staff, had an especially powerful impact on the employees' role orientation. The content of the information they were given was a significant factor in reducing role ambiguity and conflict. The authors note that institutional socialization tactics are useful for making new hires part of the organizational culture. An alternative approach is individualized socialization, which promotes innovative role orientation. This offers employees opportunities to exercise discretion in changing role requirements. For example, programmers may be given the autonomy to develop their own coding styles instead of being told to follow predefined coding standards.

Industry reports suggest that both institutional and individual socialization can be valuable for gaining the commitment of IT staff. A major complaint has been that IT employees outside of the high technology sector feel excluded from the core organizational culture. Institutional socialization can break down the traditional barrier between management and IT and clarify the role of IT in strategic operations (Fisher, 2000; Hopkins, 1998; McEachern, 2001; Zetlin, 2001). On the other hand, individual socialization can be used to validate the autonomy and creativity IT professionals desire. Smits et al. (1993) caution that due to their introversion and low interpersonal orientation, IT professionals may present a challenge for managers seeking to socialize them. With the predominance of teamwork, this may no longer be a problem. In fact, the most creative teams boast autonomy and cohesion (Amabile, 1997). What may be required is a delicate balance of institutional and individual socialization so that IT professionals can perceive themselves as valued members of the organization without feeling any impingement on their professional integrity and autonomy.

Recent Research: Empirical and Anecdotal Reports

This section presents current research drawn from the technology field, anecdotal reports by IT professionals and industry experts, and the "best practices" that are used to effectively retain IT talent.

Organizational Restructuring

In the unfolding model of job turnover, one type of shock that precipitates decisions about leaving is organizational restructuring (Lee et al., 1996). Most research on the effects of restructuring focuses on large established companies that have undergone major organizational transformation typically involving the elimination of management levels and the implementation of cross-functional work teams. High technology startups have been largely ignored. For employers of sizable numbers of IT professionals, understanding the organizational characteristics that produce turnover is essential for targeting retention strategies.

Baron et al. (2001) argue that organizational models provide blueprints for understanding the structure of employment relations. Organizational ecologists theorize that organizational survival is contingent on the establishment of reliability and accountability; underlying these

50

factors are "clearly specified forms of authority and well-understood bases of exchange between members and the organization" (p. 961). Organizational economists have a similar preference for coherence although their focus is on the importance of rational and distinctive HR systems. Although it is widely recognized that organizational inertia results when organizations are resistant to change, it is also accepted that changes in the fundamental nature of organizational blueprints have a disruptive effect. However, Baron et al. note that, "the destabilizing effects of fundamental organizational changes have been *assumed* [original emphasis] more than tested in organizational research" (p. 962).

The researchers selected Silicon Valley startups for their study for two basic reasons: "the acute shortage of scientific, technical, and engineering talent facing these organizations; and the fact that, for many technology startups, employee turnover risks losing the firm's most precious asset, its human capital" (Baron et al., 2001, p. 962). The study is part of the Stanford Project on Emerging Companies (SPEC). The researchers monitored more than 100 firms between 1991 and 1995. A variety of research strategies were used to examine the evolution of the subject firms; in all cases included in this study, changes to the original model were initiated by the founder. The companies followed five basic models that encompassed the founder's primary attachment, the criteria for selecting employees, and the method of coordination and control:

1. *Star:* the founder's attachment is to work, employees are selected for skills, and a professional culture shapes control and coordination.

2. *Engineering:* the attachment is work, employees are chosen for skills, and coordination/control is peer/cultural (informal).

3. *Commitment*: the attachment is love, employees are chosen for fit, and coordination/control is peer/cultural.

4. *Bureaucracy:* the attachment is work, employees are chosen for skills, and coordination/control is formal.

5. *Autocracy:* the attachment is money, employees are selected for skills, and coordination/control is direct.

The most prominent finding was that changing from a blueprint model to a non-traditional model (one that did not fit any of the identified types) was more disruptive than changing from one model to another (Baron et al., 2001). This effect was especially pronounced if the original model was the star or commitment. Overall, the influence of model changes on turnover was contingent upon the initial model and the subsequent form. Abandoning either an autocratic or bureaucratic model reduced turnover, whereas moving toward either one increased turnover. This finding is not surprising given the type of dynamic and fluid organizations that typically support creativity. Moving from an engineering model to a bureaucracy had the weakest effect on turnover. In fact, the engineering model was the most compatible with other organizational models and has a prominent place in Silicon Valley. The most glaring contrasts were between autocracy, which generated the highest turnover, and commitment, which boasted the lowest.

In general, turnover increased with the duration of time since the company received venture capital, but tended to abate after going public. Baron et al. (2001) propose that the process of going public can be disruptive to organizational functioning, which contributes to turnover. However, the prospect of stock options, which typically can be exercised three to five years following the initial public offering, can be a strong inducement to stay. In fact, references to stock options as a retention tactic are ubiquitous in industry magazines published in the late 1990s. Prior to the dot.com crash, stock options became less powerful as an enticement because IT workers came to expect them as an essential reward. They are more valuable as part of an overall effort to create an attractive, stimulating work environment (Zetlin, 2001), reflecting Amabile's (1997) concept of synergy between intrinsic and extrinsic rewards.

Baron et al. (2001) observed that the more times a company changed from the original model, the more new employees were on its payroll. The researchers propose that the effect was caused by an exodus of its original employees. Not unexpectedly, high turnover had a negative impact on productivity and revenues.

Intrinsic Versus Extrinsic Rewards

Longenecker and Scazzero (2003) surveyed 211 IT managers in manufacturing and service industries to examine whether they were considering leaving their jobs and if so, what factors contributed to turnover intentions and to turnover in their staff. Organizational factors had a stronger influence on intentions to leave than technical issues. Nearly half (46%) contemplated leaving their current job due to inadequate allocation of resources and staff. The next strongest influences were a better job opportunity or salary (42%) or a "bad boss" (39%). Longenecker and Scazzero conceptualize these factors as a "pull" and a "push" to leave. Job stress and work overload were cited by 37%, lack of advancement opportunities by 35%, and lack of recognition in an unfavorable organizational culture by 30%. Additional problems included lack of teamwork and cooperation, professional stagnation, job demands that impinge on personal time, and internal politics and in-fighting.

In reference to the consequences of turnover among IT managers, the most prominent response was negative impact on attaining performance goals (34%), followed by communication breakdowns, loss of direction and focus, and increases in unresolved problems. The managers also cited problems with morale and motivation, increases in stress and workload, and damage to teamwork and cooperation (Longenecker & Scazzero, 2003). Heading the list of factors that enhance retention was "challenging and stimulating work," cited by 51% of the sample. Second was an organizational culture that fostered loyalty and teamwork. Other positive factors included having organizational clout, job security, being part of a team, and advancement opportunities.

"Challenging and stimulating work" is almost invariably given high priority in surveys of IT workers. In the *InformationWeek* salary survey it was not salary that took first place but challenge, responsibility, and "job atmosphere" that topped base pay as the most important factors impacting job satisfaction (Meares & Sargent, 1999). Quality of life issues, job stability, and opportunities to gain cutting edge skills were also highly regarded. Meares and Sargent noted that the *InformationWeek* findings were consistent with results from a survey conducted by researchers at Drexel and Rider Universities "that indicates IT workers tend to rate career development and non-monetary compensation as more important to their job satisfaction than money" (p. 14). They add, however, that "Still, monetary compensation ranks high among the tools used by companies to recruit and train employees" (p. 14).

The technology consulting firm Synet Service Corp. organized a forum for clients to share strategies for retaining IT staff (Zemke, 2000). The panel's recommendations fall under four broad categories:

1. Design jobs to be challenging and interesting.

2. Provide recognition and praise for accomplishments.

3. Provide consistent, accurate, and timely performance feedback.

4. Adopt a flexible attitude to issues such as job assignments, work hours, and "style" issues such as work environment and dress code.

A national study of IT workers conducted by Minneapolis-based Personnel Decisions International (PDI) echoed the finding that "interesting and challenging work" was the key component of job satisfaction (Russo, 2002). An overwhelming 85.3% of respondents gave it first place. Salary was second, cited by 74.7% of the sample, followed by benefits (71.7%). A particularly notable finding was that while respondents gave high value to personal development plans designed to help them set and achieve goals, only 26.7% actually received them. Additionally, only 41.6% had access to non-technical skills that allowed them to learn more about management and business strategies.

One company that understands the crucial importance of exciting and challenging work is software developer Ariba. The first of Ariba's "Four Values," which is used to evaluate its workers and managers, is a commitment to "scary fun" (Zurier, 2000). The firm encourages employees to take risks—even to the point where it may seem doubtful that the risk will produce a successful outcome. The risk-taking environment paid off for Ariba in terms of productivity and retention. The company developed one of the first scalable Java server applications. Ariba's retention rate is not only enviable, but in Silicon Valley, improbable: of a total of 300 IT workers only one left the company voluntarily in three and one half years.

The 2001 IT Market Compensation Study, which encompassed 198 organizations (roughly 35,000 employees) was the only one to depart from the notion that stimulating work is the key to retaining IT talent. Interestingly, this survey investigated the reasons why IT employees actually quit instead of their prospective intentions. The top three reasons for IT turnover were: 1) was offered a promotion at another firm, 2) received a significant increase in base pay, and 3) lack of career advancement and professional development opportunities (Hacker, 2003).

According to Kochanski and Ledford (2001), "The key to understanding the causes of turnover is the 'employee value proposition' or EVP" (p. 33). The EVP encompasses the complete set of rewards an organization offers employees in exchange for continued employment and dedicated effort. The EVP includes both intrinsic and extrinsic rewards. These are:

1. *Direct financial rewards:* all monetary rewards.

2. *Indirect financial rewards:* benefits and perks.

3. *Career rewards:* long-term opportunities for development and advancement.

4. *Work content:* satisfaction that comes from the work itself.

5. *Affiliation:* the sense of belonging to a positive organization that reflects the employee's values.

The *Rewards of Work* study applied the EVP to the general U.S. workforce (n = 1,008) and to scientific and technical professionals specifically (n = 210) (Kochanski & Ledford, 2001). The five reward categories were important for both technical and non-technical employees. More than 60% of the scientific and technical sample awarded high value to the five types of rewards and considered them important influences on their decision to remain with an employer. Both the general and scientific and technical groups gave top priority to work content as the key factor in retention. This was especially true for the scientific and technical professionals; 75% rated it as "very important" or "extremely important" in determining their decision to stay or leave. Kochanski and Ledford noted that scientific and technical professionals placed higher importance on all five types of rewards than the general sample, proposing that this may reflect the tight labor market for their skills.

The culture of Ariba reflects the five rewards of the EVP. The company's pay is competitive, and rewards include stock options and benefits packages, as well as an array of exciting recreational activities (Zurier, 2000). Ariba exhorts employees to "leave your ego at the door" to create an environment based on teamwork and mutual respect enhanced by commitment to honesty and integrity. The company began by recruiting veteran engineers and still prefers employees with at least five years of experience. They seek out "generalists" who can learn from senior staff and develop skills in an environment of dynamic change and rapid obsolescence.

The preference for generalists distinguishes Ariba from many technology firms. One reason that some employers do not offer training is that they seek out candidates who have specific skills; given the short life span of hot skills and the availability of workers who possess them, they see little reason to retrain their IT staff (Meares & Sargent, 1999). Furthermore, some companies do not perceive a need to retain experienced IT staff. They contend that an IT professional's price to performance ratio declines after several years of experience when salary increases make them less cost-effective than a younger employer with a lower salary (Khosrowpour & Subramanian, 1996).

In the long run, the lack of respect for professional expertise generates higher costs in turnover than it saves in salaries. An *InformationWeek* article challenging the assumption of an IT labor shortage summed up the attitude that causes many IT professionals (including those the company might want to retain) to seek new employment: "The vast majority of companies do little to fill IT positions or reassign senior people—they treat filling IT jobs like buying PCs, looking to fill a specific spec sheet for the lowest price" (Meares & Sargent, 1999, p. 11).

The *Rewards of Work* study was supplemented by an online survey of members of the Industrial Research Institute (IRI) sponsored by the IRI and Sibson Consulting (which co-sponsored the larger survey). The IRI/Sibson study investigated the most effective solutions to turnover and job enrichment emerged as one of the top five solutions. Kochanski and Ledford (2001) commented "In most cases, staff don't quit a company, they quit a job. Improving job design is one of the least used, yet most effective ways to reduce turnover in the long-run" (p. 37). This is one area where outsourcing can have a favorable impact on retention. Outsourcing mundane tasks frees IT professionals to work on the creative projects they crave (McEachern, 2001). In fact, the job redesign tactics suggested by Kochanski and Ledford (2001), such as outsourcing routine tasks and making it easy for staff to work on a variety of projects, have been adopted by innovative financial firms as well as by R&D. The IRI members also sought opportunities to participate in spin-offs or new ventures. Stated succinctly, "This approach allows staff who are attracted to the excitement of a startup to experience it without leaving the company" (p. 37).

One significant finding of the IRI/Sibson survey strongly supports the concept of breaking down boundaries between management and IT. In the survey of IT managers, a bad boss had a particularly powerful impact on the intention to leave (Longenecker & Scazzero, 2003). Kochanski and Ledford (2001) have observed that in many technical firms, "notoriously bad managers" are ignored either because they have technical expertise or are so difficult to work with; no one wants to approach them. When the manager finally leaves (either voluntarily or involuntarily), "In almost all cases we have seen, the loss of the bad manager's expertise is far exceeded by the better retention and contribution of other staff" (p. 37). Although bad managers are often IT employees who are prized for their technical skills, a manager with no technical knowledge can have an equally adverse effect: "In most cases, a purely administrative manager is ill-equipped to prevent turnover of scientific and technical staff" (p. 37). Hopkins (1998) contends that the dichotomy between IT and management staff inevitably undermines productivity and performance.

CSX Technology effectively bridged the gap between management and IT by offering bonuses to supervisors based on retention rates in their departments and offering expanded career opportunities to IT staff (Sanminiatelli, 2000). With techniques such as these embedded in an aggressive retention program, the company reduced turnover among its 600 IT professionals from 23% in 1998 to less than 14% in 2000.

Additional solutions to turnover disclosed by the IRI/Sibson survey include providing a flexible work-life balance, offering competitive pay, and basing rewards incentive on job performance (Kochanski & Ledford, 2001). These tactics, along with those previously discussed, are consistent with Ariba's Four Values (Zurier, 2000) and are an integral part of the cultures created by the companies targeted as best places to work in IT (Zetlin, 2001).

Conclusion

Turnover among IT professionals is endemic, although the situation may have abated somewhat with the decline in the economy. During the late 1990s, companies enticed IT staff with extravagant salaries and stock options. Although money is a consistent factor in IT turnover and retention, it is generally less important than exciting and challenging work assignments, professional development and training, and rewards and recognition for professional expertise. Outside of the high technology sector, these qualities are frequently lacking. In particular, financial firms have traditionally relied on their high status and high salary offerings to attract IT talent only to have them leave when they are given mundane assignments and treated with minimal respect. Companies that have effectively reversed turnover pay careful attention to the personal and professional needs of IT staff through rewards based incentives, training and development opportunities, and flexible working conditions. Younger workers (who are most likely to leave) place especially high priority on achieving a comfortable work-life balance.

A persistent threat to retention is the traditional separation of IT and management. Some IT professionals have a managerial bent, while others prefer to refine their technical skills and deploy them on challenging projects. Failure to align IT with strategic management is a cause of job dissatisfaction for both groups. IT staff do not always understand their roles in the organization, while lack of knowledge of IT leads management to undervalue their essential contributions. Companies cited for best practices almost invariably have mechanisms that align management and IT, frequently offering employees opportunities to choose from management or IT tracks.

Organizational restructuring, downsizing, and outsourcing are structural factors that adversely impact retention. Many IT professionals, especially younger workers, tend to view *all* employment as temporary. Although rampant downsizing has produced this attitude in employees across ages and sectors, IT is unique in that frequent job hopping is perceived as an asset instead of a stigma. In fact, many IT workers view new jobs as training grounds for acquiring hot skills, which they are prepared to deploy elsewhere in view of a better offer. IT is also unique in the number of unsolicited job offers skilled professionals receive, which may motivate them to leave even if they are fairly satisfied with the current job.

Despite the powerful impact of a tight job market for IT workers with hot skills, the remarkable reduction in turnover enjoyed by firms that work to create a stimulating, group endeavor and comfortable work environment with ample opportunities for professional growth attests to the fact that turnover cannot be explained by the influence of external forces. Redesigning job and workplace features to support the needs for creativity, autonomy, challenge, and recognition that are characteristic of IT professionals, in conjunction with competitive pay and benefits packages, and quality of life options, such as flex-time and telecommuting, are key to recruiting and retaining talented IT staff.

This chapter presented an in-depth literature review of theoretical models, as well as empirical research and anecdotal reports by IT professionals and industry experts as it relates to turnover and turnover intention. The next chapter, Chapter Three, describes the research methodology, theoretical path model, and web survey in support of the goals identified in Chapter One. Additionally, hypotheses, variables and data analysis techniques are presented.

CHAPTER THREE: METHODOLOGY

The purpose of this study is to investigate the array of factors that influence job satisfaction and turnover intentions among software developers. The existing body of research has identified a number of factors that impact job satisfaction and turnover intentions among IT employees. This study is designed to explore the dynamic interaction of these factors through the analysis of data collected via a web survey.

The purpose of this chapter is to describe the research methodology that was used to answer the research questions as described in Chapter One. The research questions, research instrument, theoretical path model, hypothesis, variables, and data analysis techniques are all described in detail.

Research Questions

Two research questions provide the basis of the study:

1. Which job characteristic variables contribute to the various dimensions of job satisfaction among software developers?

2. Which job satisfaction dimensions contribute to turnover intention among software developers?

To answer each of these questions, several aspects of each software developer's job and several aspects of job satisfaction were selected. The hypotheses to be tested relate to the individual relationships between various job characteristics and the various job satisfaction variables.

Hypotheses

The model in Figure 1 was examined using the primary measure of turnover intention. The hypotheses tested are included under the two research questions:

Research question 1. Which job characteristic variables contribute to the various dimensions of job satisfaction among software developers?

The null hypotheses tested were:

1. The level of organizational commitment to software developer training does not affect the various measures of job satisfaction.

2. The number of programmers employed at the respondent's organization does not affect the various measures of job satisfaction.

3. The level of user contact does not affect the various measures of job satisfaction.

4. Job classification does not affect the various measures of job satisfaction.

5. The variety of skills required for an individual's job does not affect the various measures of job satisfaction.

6. The level of task identity does not affect job satisfaction.

7. The level of task significance does not affect job satisfaction.

8. The level of autonomy does not affect job satisfaction.

9. The amount of feedback regarding job performance does not affect job satisfaction.

Figure 1. Theoretical path model

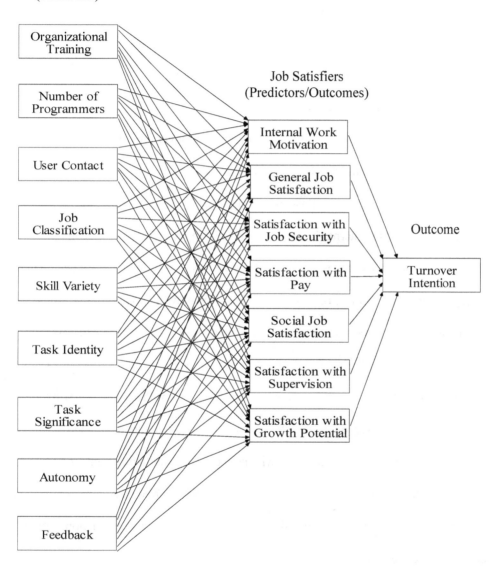

Job Characteristics
(Predictors)

Organizational
Training

Number of
Programmers

User Contact

Job
Classification

Skill Variety

Task Identity

Task
Significance

Autonomy

Feedback

Job Satisfiers
(Predictors/Outcomes)

Internal Work
Motivation

General Job
Satisfaction

Satisfaction with
Job Security

Satisfaction with
Pay

Social Job
Satisfaction

Satisfaction with
Supervision

Satisfaction with
Growth Potential

Outcome

Turnover
Intention

Research question 2. Which job satisfaction dimensions contribute to turnover intention among software developers?

10. The level of internal work motivation does not affect turnover intention.

11. The level of general job satisfaction does not affect turnover intention.

12. The level of job security satisfaction does not affect turnover intention.

13. The level of satisfaction with pay does not affect turnover intention.

14. The level of social job satisfaction does not affect turnover intention.

15. The level of satisfaction with supervision does not affect turnover intention.

16. The level of job growth satisfaction does not affect turnover intention.

Research Design

This project utilized an Internet-based survey hosted on the web server at Dolphin Software Inc. A survey methodology was selected because it was desired to collect data on many individuals regarding a large number of constructs. This is the only methodology that would allow querying numerous software developers without being restricted to readers of a particular technical journal, developers utilizing a particular technology, or those frequenting only a single forum, etc. An invitation to take the survey was posted on the sites of Programming/Software Development Forums and Newsgroups. The study was designed to capture a large pool of programmers, software engineers, and analysts with no inclusion criteria other than job title and job tasks. All respondent information was acquired through self-reported data. The data derived from the survey was analyzed and is discussed in the next two chapters in conjunction with the existing body of related research.

Selection of Subjects

The sample for this study was drawn from a global population of IT professionals whose titles are Programmer, Software Engineer, or Programmer Analyst. Survey respondents were recruited via the Internet by posting an invitation to participate in the survey on a series of Programming/Software Development Forums and Newsgroups. This method was utilized to attract a broad spectrum of software developers who use a variety of technologies and computer languages. The forums and newsgroups are typically frequented by individuals representing a wide range of educational backgrounds, professional experience, and technical skills. The Internet provides an efficient medium for recruiting software developers as well as expanding the pool of respondents beyond organizational and geographic boundaries.

Instrumentation

The web survey instrument is contained in Appendix C and has two components. The first part was designed to gather basic demographic information. Additionally, this section contains questions relating to employment, as well as data on some specific characteristics of each respondent's job, organization, and turnover intention. A description of the variables in this section that are included in the inferential analyses follows.

Respondents were asked whether they would like a copy of the survey results upon completion. Those who would like a copy were asked for a valid e-mail address, and all respondents were assured of complete anonymity.

Variables

The variables for this study fall into two categories called job characteristics and job satisfaction, and are described below.

Job Characteristics

Based on the literature review, several potential job characteristics were included in the survey. The first four are specific to software developers, while the last five are from the Job Diagnostic Survey (JDS; Hackman & Oldham, 1985), a general measure to assess job characteristics common to most jobs. The JDS was designed to provide a standardized measure of the key components of an individual's job as they relate to job satisfaction. A revised version of the scale was presented by Idaszak and Drascgow (1987) in which the revision of previously reverse-scored items resulted in scales with better psychometric properties. The revised version of the scale was employed in the present study.

The following software developer job characteristics were selected specifically for the current study:

Organizational training. The level of commitment of the organization to providing training to software developers may impact certain aspects of job satisfaction. This construct is assessed with a single questionnaire item (Part 1, Item 16) that assesses the financial commitment of the organization to training software developers: "How committed is your organization to providing software development training?" Possible responses are (a) no money, (b) a little money, (c) a reasonable amount of money, (d) a lot of money, or (e) unlimited money. This data is used to test hypothesis number 1.

Number of programmers. The number of software developers in the organization may be related to job satisfaction. This is assessed with a single questionnaire item (Part 1, Item 6): "Number of software developers/analysts in current organization." The respondent is then asked to enter a number. This data has been used to test hypothesis number 2.

User contact. The degree of contact that the software developer has with the ultimate users of work products may be related to job satisfaction. This construct is assessed with a single questionnaire item (Part 1, Item 10): "How often do you work directly with the users of the software you develop?" Possible responses are (a) never, (b) rarely, (c) sometimes, (d) frequently, and (e) always. This data is used to test hypothesis number 3.

Job classification. Whether a software developer is primarily a programmer or primarily an analyst may impact job satisfaction. This is assessed with a single questionnaire item (Part 1, Item 13) which asks respondents to select their primary job description with the following options: (a) write code, test, debug, documentation, (b) problem analysis, design solutions, write a little code, work with users. Choice (a) will be selected by respondents that are primarily programmers and choice (b) will be selected by analysts. This data has been used to test hypothesis number 4.

The last five job characteristics are part of the JDS:

Skill variety. Hackman and Oldham (1975) define skill variety as "The degree to which a job requires a variety of different activities in carrying out the work, which involve the use of a number of different skills and talents of the employee" (p. 161). Skill variety is assessed with a three-item scale (Part 2, Section 1, Item 4; Part 2, Section 2, Items 1 and 5). This data is used to test hypothesis number 5.

Task identity. Task identity relates to the extent to which an individual's job results in a "whole" product, as opposed to merely a piece of some larger entity. Three items from the JDS are used to assess task identity (Part 2, Section 1, Item 3; Part 2, Section 2, Items 3 and 11). This data has been used to test hypothesis number 6.

68

Task significance. The perceived importance of one's job, that is, the extent to which it is perceived by the employee to have a real impact on the world, is assessed with 3 questionnaire items (Part 2, Section 1, Item 5; Part 2, Section 2, Items 8 and 14). This data is used to test hypothesis number 7.

Autonomy. The degree of freedom or independence in one's job, in terms of scheduling and deciding exactly how to carry out the assigned tasks, is assessed with three questionnaire items (Part 2, Section 1, Item 2; Part 2, Section 2, Items 9 and 13). This data has been used to test hypothesis number 8.

Feedback. The clarity and directness of the information about job performance (from the work itself) is assessed with three questionnaire items (Part 2, Section 1, Item 7; Part 2, Section 2, Items 4 and 12). This data is used to test hypothesis number 9.

Job Satisfaction Scales

The second part of the survey contains questions about job satisfaction from the JDS.

Internal work motivation. This domain assesses the extent to which an employee is self-motivated to perform well. Individuals who have positive feelings when they perform well will score highly on this scale, which is assessed by six questionnaire items (Part 2, Section 3, Items 1, 3, 5, and 7; Part 2, Section 5, Items 1 and 4). This data has been used to test hypothesis number 10.

General job satisfaction. This dimension assesses the extent to which the employee is satisfied or happy with the job in a broad sense. Five questionnaire items (Part 2, Section 3, Items 2, 4, and 6; Part 2, Section 5, Items 2 and 3) are used to assess this domain. This data is used to test hypothesis number 11.

Satisfaction with job security. Two questionnaire items (Part 2, Section 4, Items 1 and 11) assess the extent to which an employee feels secure that employment will be continued. This data is used to test hypothesis number 12.

Satisfaction with pay. Two questionnaire items (Part 2, Section 4, Items 2 and 9) assess the degree to which the remuneration for the work performed is considered adequate. This data has been used to test hypothesis number 13.

Social job satisfaction. Three questionnaire items (Part 2, Section 4, Items 4, 7, and 12) assess the extent to which an employee is satisfied with the social relationships associated with the job. This data is used to test hypothesis number 14.

Satisfaction with supervision. Three questionnaire items (Part 2, Section 4, Items 5, 8, and 14) assess the degree to which the employee feels that the superiors deal fairly with employees. This data has been used to test hypothesis number 15.

Satisfaction with growth potential. Four questionnaire items (Part 2, Section 4, Items 3, 6, and 10, and 13) deal with the employee's perception of the potential for upward mobility. This data is used to test hypothesis number 16.

Turnover Intention

In addition to job characteristics and job satisfaction, turnover intention was central to the study. Turnover intention is assessed in two ways. The primary method is with the questionnaire item (Part 1, Item 21): How long in years do you currently plan to continue working with your current organization? Additionally, an alternative question (Part 1, Item 20) asks: How would you characterize your intentions to seek a new job with a different organization? The following response options are available: (a) I'm ready to go, (b) I could be lured away easily, (c) I may leave but am not desperate to go, (d) I am not presently considering leaving this organization, and (e) I'd have to be dragged out of here. The primary method was examined first, with the alternative providing a basis for an alternative set of analyses in the event that problems arise with the primary measure.

Procedures

Data Collection

All data was collected by means of a web survey. A hyperlink to the survey, request for participation, and all relevant information was posted on a series of software development forums and newsgroups. These include general software development forums and newsgroups such as Tek-Tips Forums, TechTalk Computer Support, and MVN Forum-Open Source Discussion Board; language specific software development forums and newsgroups, such as Java Technology Forums and Visual Basic Internet Programming Forums; and platform specific software development forums, such as Microsoft and Hewlett-Packard. The request for participation included an offer to enter the respondents into a drawing. Four respondents were selected at random from all completed surveys to receive a $50 gift certificate for Amazon.com.

The respondent's IP address was recorded in order to isolate any duplicates, ensuring that no one responded to the survey more than once. It is understood that this procedure is not foolproof. First, it may invalidate some legitimate responses, since multiple software developers could be using the same IP address. Alternately, it is possible for one person to respond to the survey multiple times from different IP addresses. To address this possibility, the act of completing the survey created a cookie that was used to discern whether anyone was attempting to answer the survey twice from the same computer.

71

Data Processing and Analysis

Data Processing

The survey instrument was a series of web pages hosted at Dolphin Software Inc. in Lake Oswego, Oregon. Each page of the survey validated the data prior to completing the current page and progressing to the next page. Any data that was missing was immediately flagged and the survey respondent received instant feedback that this page must be completed in its entirety before progressing to the next page. This guaranteed that no surveys had any missing data. All data received via the web survey was stored in a Microsoft SQL database. The goal was to have a minimum of 200 respondents, and it was originally estimated that the survey would need to remain available for a period of two weeks. After one week, the goal was met and the survey continued to gather data for the second week. By the end of the second week, over 300 surveys had been completed.

After the two week period had ended, the survey was removed from the web server and filtering the data commenced. Duplicate responses based on originating IP address were ignored. Job titles that did not fall into the category of Software Developers were also ignored. Filtering free-form entry of job titles became a manual task performed by the researcher, which required a judgment call that a job title such as Applications Programmer falls under the broad heading of Software Developer, but is not one of the selectable job titles. Once all data was filtered, the data from the remaining qualifying surveys was exported into Excel and massaged in a manner that allowed direct importation into the two computer programs described next, that were used for data analysis.

Data Analysis

Both descriptive and inferential statistical methods were employed. Descriptive statistics

(percentages, means, and standard deviations) were computed using the Statistical Package for

the Social Sciences (SPSS, Inc., 2002), a general-purpose data analysis program. SPSS was used

to characterize the sample in terms of demographic characteristics, job characteristics, job

satisfaction, and turnover intention. Correlations are presented between all of the study variables

prior to the main set of inferential analyses. In addition, reliability analyses (Cronbach's α) were

conducted for the JDS scales. Reliability coefficients range from 0 to 1, and Aiken (2000, p. 88)

reported that values between .60 and .70 are adequate for research purposes. The primary

inferential technique employed was path analysis. All path analyses were conducted in the

Analysis of Moment Structures (AMOS; SmallWaters, Inc., 2001) computer program. AMOS is

a general-purpose data-modeling program that uses a structural equation-modeling framework.

Path analysis is an extension of multiple regression analysis in which selected variables can be

employed as both predictor variables and outcome variables. In the present study, it is the job

satisfaction variables that take this dual role: The various job satisfaction variables were modeled

as outcomes of the job characteristic variables and as predictors of turnover intention. The

research questions that were addressed in the present study are represented in Figure 1. On the

left side of the figure are the job characteristic variables, the first four of which are assessed in

Part 1 of the survey instrument, while the last five are from the JDS. The figure does not show

(for simplicity) the double-headed arrows between each pair of job characteristic variables,

which indicate that they are correlated with each other. The job characteristic variables are

connected to the job satisfaction variables in the middle of the diagram by single headed arrows indicating that the latter depend on the former. The turnover intention variable, in turn, is predicted by the job satisfaction variables.

Seven tests of each of the first nine hypotheses were performed corresponding to the seven components of job satisfaction. Although this resulted in a large number of hypotheses to be tested (and a busy figure), it allowed for a highly detailed examination of the relationships between job characteristics, job satisfaction, and turnover intention. For example, it may be the case that the job characteristic of autonomy is only related to satisfaction with supervision and satisfaction with pay, but not with the other components of satisfaction, a finding that would be unreachable if a single overall measure of job satisfaction were employed. Each null hypothesis was tested by examining the statistical significance of the regression coefficient for the path from the particular predictor variable to the particular outcome variable. For example, null hypothesis number 10 was tested by determining the statistical significance of the path from intrinsic work motivation to turnover intention. An α level of .05 was used for all null hypothesis tests.

All of these hypotheses were tested in what are essentially eight multiple regression analyses, one for each variable that has single-headed arrows pointing toward it in Figure 1. For example, one regression analysis was computed with intrinsic work motivation as the criterion variable and the nine job characteristics as the predictors. Additionally, a second regression analysis was conducted with general job satisfaction as the criterion variable and the nine job characteristics as the predictors, and so on until the last one which was conducted with turnover intention as the criterion variable and the seven job satisfaction variables as the predictors.

The use of path analysis rather than eight individual regression analyses produced results that are in many ways identical, but allowed for the estimation of indirect effects (for example, the effect of autonomy on turnover intention through general satisfaction). Because turnover intention is the ultimate outcome measure of the study (and job satisfaction is seen only as a tool with which to reduce turnover intention), the indirect effects of the job characteristics on turnover intention are critical. For example, if the standardized effect (beta) of autonomy on general satisfaction is .50, and the standardized effect of general satisfaction on turnover intention is .25, then the product (.25*.50) = .125 is the standardized indirect effect of autonomy on turnover intention through general satisfaction. The sum of all of the indirect effects for a given job characteristic indicates the overall effect of that characteristic on turnover intention. Because the job characteristics are directly alterable (e.g., more user contact or autonomy can be designed into a job), the effect that those changes would have on turnover intention, as a result of enhancing job satisfaction, is critical.

Summary

This chapter described the research technique, web survey, theoretical path model, and how the research was conducted in support of the goals identified in Chapter One and shown to be lacking through the review of the relevant literature in Chapter Two. This chapter also presented the hypotheses and variables that were developed to answer the research questions. The next chapter, Chapter Four, will describe the findings of this study through the analysis of the data provided by the survey instrument.

CHAPTER FOUR: FINDINGS

This chapter presents a detailed discussion of the descriptive and inferential statistical data analysis. Bivariate correlations are presented, as well as multiple regression analysis allowing for a comparison between the two results. All computer generated statistical output is included in addition to a detailed data analysis for each hypothesis including the indirect effects of job characteristics on turnover intention.

Descriptive Statistics

Background Variables

In order to provide background information on the 326 respondents who provided valid data, descriptive statistics were calculated. The mean age of the respondents was 36.79 years, with a standard deviation of 10.42. The youngest respondent was 20 years old and the oldest was 63. The number of years as a software developer ranged from 1 to 40 years with a mean of 12.40 years (standard deviation = 9.11). The number of years with the current organization ranged from 1 to 38 years with a mean of 5.84 years (standard deviation = 6.66). The number of years in their current position ranged from 1 to 30 years with a mean of 4.23 years (standard deviation = 4.58).

Table 1 contains frequencies and percentages for all categorical background variables. As can be seen, the sample was predominantly male (91.7%). Respondent income was broadly distributed, with 23.6% earning less than $40,000 per year (the sum of the two lowest categories), and 27% earning more than $80,000 per year. Somewhat surprisingly, almost a third of the sample (33.1%) did not have a college degree, and over one-quarter (25.7%) had a college

Table 1

Descriptive Statistics for Background Variables

	Frequency	Percentage
Gender		
Male	299	91.7
Female	27	8.3
Income		
Below 30K	45	13.8
30K – 40K	32	9.8
40K – 50K	42	12.9
50K – 60K	45	13.8
60K – 70K	36	11.0
70K – 80K	38	11.7
Above 80K	88	27.0
Education		
High school diploma or less	22	6.7
Some college	86	26.4
Completed a computer-related bachelor's degree	83	25.5
Completed a bachelor's degree in another discipline	48	14.7
Completed a computer-related graduate degree	51	15.6
Completed a graduate degree in another discipline	36	11.0
Primary Job Title		
Programmer	57	17.5
Software engineer	87	26.7
Programmer/Analyst	100	30.7
Systems analyst	21	6.4
Other	61	18.7
Level of Technological Development at Organization		
A clay tablet	2	.6
Pencil and paper	10	3.1
Barely electronic	28	8.6
Fairly current	203	62.3
State-of-the-art	83	25.5
Work Preference		
Heavy design/analysis	33	10.1
Moderate design/analysis	49	15.0

	Frequency	Percentage
Some design/analysis	40	12.3
Just write code	16	4.9
All phases of the software development life cycle	188	57.7
Understanding of Business Impact of Work		
I'm clueless	6	1.8
A little	23	7.1
Somewhat	46	14.1
Quite a bit	162	49.7
Completely	89	27.3
Visibility Within the Organization		
Anonymous	7	2.1
Low visibility	45	13.8
Moderate visibility	80	24.5
High visibility	73	22.4
Everyone knows me	121	37.1
Development Process Within the Organization		
Chaotic	62	19.0
Semi-structured	162	49.7
Methodology defined	73	22.4
SDLC	22	6.7
Very formal	7	2.1
How Was the Current Position Obtained		
Applied for an advertised position	82	25.2
Hired through a headhunter	28	8.6
Promoted/transferred from a non-programming position	30	9.2
Promoted/transferred from a programming position	49	15.0
Recruited by the organization	100	30.7
Other	37	11.3
Primary Duty		
Developing new systems	84	25.8
An equal mix of new and existing systems	175	53.7
Maintaining/enhancing existing systems	56	17.2
Other	11	3.4

degree (either a bachelor's degree or a graduate degree) in a field other than computers. The most frequent response to job title was programmer/analyst, followed by software engineer.

The majority of the sample (62.3%) reported that the level of technology at their organization was fairly current. The majority (57.7%) also preferred to be involved in all aspects of software development. Approximately half of the respondents (49.7%) felt that they knew quite a bit about the business impact of their work, while only 8.9% reported that they were clueless or knew only a little about it. The respondents generally felt that they had a high degree of visibility within the organization, with 37.1% reporting that they were known by everyone in the organization. The development process at the respondents' organizations was most frequently referred to as semi-structured (48.7%), while only 2.1% stated that it was very formal. The respondents most frequently arrived at their current position from outside the organization either through recruitment (30.7%) or by applying for an advertised position (25.2%). The majority of the respondents (53.7%) reported that they worked on both new and existing software.

Job Characteristics

Means and standard deviations for the job characteristic variables are provided in the top section of Table 2. The first four job characteristics are from Part 1 of the survey while the last five are from the Job Diagnostic Survey. The original values for number of programmers ranged from 1 to 4000 with a mean of 91.18 (standard deviation = 347.58) and a median of 8, indicating a highly positively skewed distribution. Therefore, five approximately equal categories were formed in the following manner: 1 or 2 programmers = '1' (n=73); 3 to 5 programmers = '2' (n=64); 6 to 12 programmers = '3' (n=59); 15 to 50 programmers = '4' (71); and more than 50 programmers = '5' (n=59).

Table 2

Descriptive Statistics for Path Analysis Variables

	Mean	SD	Item Mean	Hackman & Oldham Item Mean for Professional/Technical
Job Characteristics Scales				
Organizational Training	2.30	.96		
Number of Developers[1]	2.94	1.43		
Work with Users	3.44	1.21		
Job Classification[2]	.48	.50		
Skill Variety	16.61	3.34	5.54	5.4
Task Identity	16.40	3.47	5.47	5.1
Task Significance	15.35	4.21	5.12	5.6
Autonomy	17.25	3.23	5.75	5.4
Feedback	15.39	3.54	5.13	5.1
Job Satisfaction Scales				
Internal Work Motivation	32.80	5.19	5.47	5.8
General Job Satisfaction	23.33	4.43	4.66	4.9
Satisfaction with Job Security	9.28	3.31	4.64	5.0
Satisfaction with Pay	9.28	3.31	4.64	4.4
Social Job Satisfaction	15.44	3.46	5.14	5.5
Satisfaction with Supervision	13.66	4.73	4.55	4.9
Satisfaction with Job Growth	21.13	4.96	5.28	5.1

Note. [1]This is the recoded version of the number of programmers; [2]Coded as '0' = Programmer, '1' = Analyst. The Item Mean column represents the mean divided by the number of survey questions relating to that job characteristic or job satisfier.

The mean and standard deviation of the transformed variable are presented in Table 2. The sample was made up of slightly more programmers (n=169; 51.8%) than analysts (n=157; 48.2%), and this variable was coded as '0' = programmer, '1' = analysts for analysis. Each of the job characteristic scales from the JDS is composed of the same number of items (i.e. three), indicating that the scores can be compared. The Job Diagnostic Survey characteristic that was most highly rated by the sample was autonomy (mean item score = 17.25/3 = 5.75). The mean item score is comparable to that reported by Hackman and Oldham (1980, p. 317) for a sample of professional/technical workers (5.4). The least highly rated characteristic was task significance (mean item score = 15.35/3 = 5.12), which was somewhat lower than that from Hackman and Oldham's professional/technical sample (5.6). The standardized means are displayed in Table 2 with Hackman and Oldham's professional/technical sample means.

Job Satisfaction Scales

Means and standard deviations for the job satisfaction scales of the Job Diagnostic Survey are presented in the lower section of Table 2. Again, the standardized means are displayed in Table 2 with Hackman and Oldham's professional/technical sample means. The job satisfaction scale with the highest mean item score was internal work motivation (32.80/6 = 5.47), which is slightly lower than the mean item score for Hackman and Oldham's (1980) sample of professional/technical workers (5.8). The job satisfaction scale with the lowest mean item score was satisfaction with supervision (13.66/3 = 4.55), again slightly lower than that reported for Hackman and Oldham's professional/technical sample (4.9).

Reliability of the Job Diagnostic Survey Scores

Cronbach's α (internal consistency) reliability coefficients were calculated for the 12

scores from the JDS, and these are presented in Table 3. The reliability coefficients range from

.74 to .92. As noted in Chapter Three, reliability coefficients of .60 or higher are considered

adequate for research purposes (Aiken, 2000, p. 88), so these reliabilities are fairly high,

especially considering that some of the scales have as few as two items.

Inferential Statistics

Operationalization of Turnover Intention

As noted in Chapter 3, two measures of turnover intention were included in the survey.

The first was a five-point Likert scale (Item 20, Part 1 in Appendix C) ranging from "I'm ready

to go" to "I'd have to be dragged out of here." Second, was the estimated number of years the

respondent planned on working with the current company. The respondents were also asked if

the estimated number of years they planned on working were until retirement. Of the 326

subjects, 87 (26.7%) stated that their estimate of the number of years were, in fact, based on

years to retirement. Therefore, some respondents who gave small estimates of the number of

years they planned to be with the current company, which would apparently indicate high

turnover intention, actually provided a small estimate because they were nearing retirement.

Consequently, the number of years that the respondents planned on staying with the current

company were not a good measure of turnover intention. Based on this finding, the Likert scale

of turnover intention was used as the outcome measure in all subsequent analyses.

Table 3

Reliability Coefficients for the Job Diagnostic Survey Scales

	Cronbach's α
Job Characteristic Scales	
Skill Variety	.79
Task Identity	.76
Task Significance	.84
Autonomy	.86
Feedback	.82
Job Satisfaction Scales	
Internal Work Motivation	.80
General Job Satisfaction	.84
Satisfaction with Job Security	.92
Satisfaction with Pay	.88
Social Job Satisfaction	.74
Satisfaction with Supervision	.89
Satisfaction with Job Growth	.84

Correlations Between Job Characteristics

Table 4 presents the correlations between the job characteristic scores. Again, the first four questions are from the single questionnaire items in Part 1 of the survey, while the last five are from the JDS. For all of the job characteristics except number of programmers and job classification, higher scores are considered better than lower scores. For example, it is better to have a large amount of organizational training than not, better to have task identity than not, etc. For job classification, recall that this variable was coded as '0' for programmers and '1' for analysts; therefore, the positive correlations with other variables indicate that those with higher scores on job classification (i.e. analysts) tend to have higher scores on the other job characteristics variables. For number of programmers, the correlations with the other job characteristics tend to be negative, indicating that respondents from organizations with a large number of programmers tended to rate the other job characteristics as less positive (e.g., to have less work with users, task identity, autonomy, and feedback). The exception is that respondents from organizations with a large number of programmers tended to have more organizational training. The other correlations in Table 4 tend to be positive, particularly with respect to the JDS scales, which range from .31 to .63.

Correlations Between Job Satisfaction Scales

The correlations between the job satisfaction measures from the JDS are shown in Table 5. All of the correlations are positive and statistically significant, indicating that individuals who are satisfied with one aspect of their jobs tend to be satisfied with other areas as well. The largest correlation (.79) is between general job satisfaction and satisfaction with job growth.

Table 4

Correlations Between the Job Characteristics

	1.	2.	3.	4.	5.	6.	7.	8.	9.
1. Organizational Training	1.0								
2. Number of Developers[1]	.14	1.0							
3. Work with Users	.15	-.18	1.0						
4. Job Classification[2]	.10	.02	.27	1.0					
5. Skill Variety	.22	-.05	.22	.19	1.0				
6. Task Identity	.06	-.21	.28	-.02	.34	1.0			
7. Task Significance	.24	-.10	.33	.19	.43	.31	1.0		
8. Autonomy	.08	-.29	.26	.11	.54	.63	.44	1.0	
9. Feedback	.26	-.13	.22	.12	.53	.46	.43	.49	1.0

Note. Correlations greater than or equal to .15 in absolute value are statistically significant at the .01 α level; Correlations greater than or equal to .11 in absolute value are statistically significant at the .05 α level. [1]This is the recoded version of the number of programmers; [2]Coded as '0' = Programmer, '1' = Analyst.

Table 5

Correlations Between the Job Satisfaction Scales

	1.	2.	3.	4.	5.	6.	7.
1. Internal Work Motivation	1.0						
2. General Job Satisfaction	.54	1.0					
3. Satisfaction with Job Security	.26	.43	1.0				
4. Satisfaction with Pay	.25	.46	.30	1.0			
5. Social Job Satisfaction	.53	.59	.39	.35	1.0		
6. Satisfaction with Supervision	.39	.66	.47	.43	.60	1.0	
7. Satisfaction with Job Growth	.61	.79	.37	.33	.60	.58	1.0

Note. All correlations are statistically significant at the .01 α level.

Correlations Between Job Characteristics and Job Satisfaction Scales

The correlations between the job characteristics and job satisfaction scales are shown in Table 6. As can be seen, many of the correlations are statistically significant (i.e. any correlation greater than or equal to .11 is statistically significant at the .05 α level) and large in magnitude. These correlations form the basis of the path analyses to be discussed in the next section and so will not be extensively discussed here. However, it is worth noting that the largest correlation between satisfaction with job growth and several of the job characteristics are among the largest. These include the correlations between job growth and skill variety (.63), autonomy (.63), feedback (.62), task identity (.47) and task significance (.47). Conversely, some of the lowest correlations were for satisfaction with pay, which was significantly correlated with only four of the job characteristics.

Turnover Intention, Job Characteristics, Job Satisfaction Scales Correlations

The correlations between turnover intention and the job characteristics and job satisfaction scales are shown in Table 7. As can be seen, 13 of the 16 correlations are statistically significant and negative, indicating that higher scores on the job characteristics and job satisfaction scales are associated with lower turnover intention, as would be expected. The only correlations that are not statistically significant are those between turnover intention and (a) number of developers, (b) work with users, and (c) job classification. The correlations tend to be stronger for the job satisfaction scales than for the job characteristics.

Prediction of Internal Work Motivation by the Job Characteristics Scales

The first job satisfaction scale examined was the internal work motivation scale. Table 8 presents the standardized regression coefficients, t-values, and p-values for the prediction of

Table 6

Correlations Between the Job Characteristics and Job Satisfaction Scales

	Job Characteristics								
	Org. Train.	Num. Dev.[1]	Work User	Job Clas.[2]	Skill Var.	Task ID	Task Sign.	Auto-nomy	Feed-back
Job Satisfaction Scales									
Internal Work Motivation	.23	.01	.21	.12	.41	.25	.40	.34	.46
General Job Satisfaction	.34	.01	.20	.11	.47	.39	.37	.45	.56
Satisfaction with Job Security	.21	.01	.18	-.10	.22	.15	.25	.23	.34
Satisfaction with Pay	.28	.16	.05	.09	.16	.02	.09	.09	.24
Social Job Satisfaction	.26	.21	.19	.12	.44	.23	.42	.32	.48
Satisfaction with Supervision	.33	.08	.05	-.04	.28	.26	.24	.29	.48
Satisfaction with Job Growth	.32	-.08	.26	.15	.63	.47	.47	.63	.62

Note. Correlations greater than or equal to .15 in absolute value are statistically significant at the .01 α level; Correlations greater than or equal to .11 in absolute value are statistically significant at the .05 α level. [1]This is the recoded version of the number of programmers; [2]Coded as '0' = Programmer, '1' = Analyst.

Table 7

Turnover Intention, Job Characteristics and Job Satisfaction Scales Correlations

	Turnover Intention
Job Characteristics	
Organizational Training	-.34
Number of Developers*[1]	-.07
Work with Users*	-.06
Job Classification*[2]	-.06
Skill Variety	-.29
Task Identity	-.17
Task Significance	-.18
Autonomy	-.23
Feedback	-.31
Job Satisfaction Scales	
Internal Work Motivation	-.26
General Job Satisfaction	-.64
Satisfaction with Job Security	-.35
Satisfaction with Pay	-.43
Social Job Satisfaction	-.39
Satisfaction with Supervision	-.49
Satisfaction with Job Growth	-.48

Note.   *All correlations except these are statistically significant at the .01 α level. [1]This is the recoded version of the number of programmers; [2]Coded as '0' = Programmer, '1' = Analyst.

Table 8

Prediction of Internal Work Motivation by the Job Characteristics Scales

Predictor Variable	β	t	p
Organizational Training	.059	1.176	.240
Number of Developers[1]	.093	1.853	.065
Work with Users	.057	1.095	.274
Job Classification[2]	-.004	-.084	.933
Skill Variety	.141	2.303	.022
Task Identity	-.015	-.243	.808
Task Significance	.178	3.146	.002
Autonomy	.071	.996	.320
Feedback	.266	4.378	<.0005

Note.   [1]This is the recoded version of the number of programmers; [2]Coded as '0' = Programmer, '1' = Analyst.

internal work motivation by the job characteristics. Overall, 29.8% of the variance in internal work motivation scores was explained by the job characteristics. Three of the job characteristics were significantly related to internal work motivation: skill variety, task significance, and feedback. All three of the standardized regression coefficients were positive, indicating that higher scores on skill variety, task significance, and feedback were associated with higher internal work motivation.

Prediction of General Job Satisfaction by the Job Characteristics Scales

The results of the prediction of general job satisfaction from the job characteristics are presented in Table 9. As can be seen, five of the job characteristics were predictive of general job satisfaction: organizational training, the number of developers, skill variety, autonomy, and feedback. Again, all of the standardized regression coefficients were positive indicating that higher scores on the predictors were associated with higher general job satisfaction. A total of 42.4% of the variance in general job satisfaction was explained by the job characteristic.

Prediction of Satisfaction with Job Security by the Job Characteristics Scales

The third job satisfaction variable was satisfaction with job security, and the results are shown in Table 10. Four of the nine job characteristics were statistically significant. The relationships between satisfaction with job security and organizational training, amount of work with users, and feedback were positive, while the relationship between job classification and satisfaction with job security was negative. Given the manner of coding job classification (i.e. '0' = programmer, '1' = analyst), this indicates that programmers were more satisfied with their job security than analysts. In total, 19.2% of the variance in satisfaction with job security was explained by the job characteristics.

91

Table 9

Prediction of General Job Satisfaction by the Job Characteristics Scales

Predictor Variable	β	t	p
Organizational Training	.181	3.999	<.0005
Number of Developers[1]	.105	2.310	.022
Work with Users	.014	.286	.775
Job Classification[2]	-.001	-.032	.974
Skill Variety	.129	2.331	.020
Task Identity	.098	1.712	.088
Task Significance	.047	.916	.360
Autonomy	.158	2.462	.014
Feedback	.309	5.614	<.0005

Note.   [1]This is the recoded version of the number of programmers; [2]Coded as '0' = Programmer, '1' = Analyst.

Table 10

Prediction of Satisfaction with Job Security by the Job Characteristics Scales

Predictor Variable	β	t	p
Organizational Training	.110	2.047	.041
Number of Developers[1]	.078	1.438	.151
Work with Users	.141	2.510	.013
Job Classification[2]	-.212	-3.975	<.0005
Skill Variety	.005	.070	.944
Task Identity	-.110	-1.615	.107
Task Significance	.090	1.482	.139
Autonomy	.129	1.695	.091
Feedback	.257	3.942	<.0005

Note.   [1]This is the recoded version of the number of programmers; [2]Coded as '0' = Programmer, '1' = Analyst.

Prediction of Satisfaction with Pay by the Job Characteristics Scales

In the examination of satisfaction with pay, three of the job characteristics were statistically significant: organizational training, number of developers, and feedback. Each of these predictors had a positive relationship with satisfaction with pay (see Table 11). In total, 14.4% of the variance in satisfaction with pay was explained by the job characteristics.

Prediction of Social Job Satisfaction by the Job Characteristics Scales

Table 12 shows that four of the job characteristic scales were associated with social job satisfaction: number of developers, skill variety, task significance, and feedback. All of the statistically significant predictors had a positive relationship with social job satisfaction, and a total of 40.0% of the variance was explained.

Prediction of Satisfaction with Supervision by the Job Characteristics Scales

In the analysis of satisfaction with supervision (see Table 13), five of the job characteristics were statistically significant: organizational training, number of developers, job classification, autonomy, and feedback. Each of the statistically significant predictors was positively associated with satisfaction with supervision except job classification, for which the relationship was negative. Again, this indicates that programmers were more satisfied with supervision than analysts. Overall, 31.9% of the variance in satisfaction with supervision was explained by the job characteristics.

Prediction of Satisfaction with Job Growth by the Job Characteristics Scales

Table 14 shows that four of the job characteristics were positively associated with satisfaction with job growth: organizational training, skill variety, autonomy, and feedback. In

Table 11

Prediction of Satisfaction with Pay by the Job Characteristics Scales

Predictor Variable	β	t	p
Organizational Training	.208	3.766	<.0005
Number of Developers[1]	.162	2.915	.004
Work with Users	.008	.135	.893
Job Classification[2]	.030	.541	.589
Skill Variety	.005	.074	.941
Task Identity	-.105	-1.507	.133
Task Significance	-.059	-.940	.348
Autonomy	.099	1.259	.209
Feedback	.224	3.335	.001

Note. [1]This is the recoded version of the number of programmers; [2]Coded as '0' = Programmer, '1' = Analyst.

Table 12

Prediction of Social Job Satisfaction by the Job Characteristics Scales

Predictor Variable	β	t	p
Organizational Training	.041	.885	.377
Number of Developers[1]	.306	6.585	<.0005
Work with Users	.068	1.410	.160
Job Classification[2]	-.017	-.368	.713
Skill Variety	.150	2.655	.008
Task Identity	-.042	-.711	.478
Task Significance	.191	3.675	<.0005
Autonomy	.103	1.565	.119
Feedback	.302	5.373	<.0005

Note. [1]This is the recoded version of the number of programmers; [2]Coded as '0' = Programmer, '1' = Analyst.

Table 13

Prediction of Satisfaction with Supervision by the Job Characteristics Scales

Predictor Variable	β	t	p
Organizational Training	.223	4.515	<.0005
Number of Developers[1]	.144	2.911	.004
Work with Users	-.057	-1.104	.270
Job Classification[2]	-.109	-2.232	.026
Skill Variety	-.029	-.475	.635
Task Identity	.027	.427	.670
Task Significance	.015	.273	.785
Autonomy	.147	2.097	.037
Feedback	.388	6.470	<.0005

Note.   [1]This is the recoded version of the number of programmers; [2]Coded as '0' = Programmer, '1' = Analyst.

97

Table 14

Prediction of Satisfaction with Job Growth by the Job Characteristics Scales

Predictor Variable	β	t	p
Organizational Training	.141	3.804	<.0005
Number of Developers[1]	.055	1.472	.142
Work with Users	.023	.592	.554
Job Classification[2]	.007	.185	.853
Skill Variety	.253	5.593	<.0005
Task Identity	.048	1.018	.309
Task Significance	.062	1.476	.141
Autonomy	.313	5.958	<.0005
Feedback	.254	5.637	<.0005

Note.   [1]This is the recoded version of the number of programmers; [2]Coded as '0' = Programmer, '1' = Analyst.

total 61.6% of the variance in satisfaction with job growth was explained by the job characteristics.

Prediction of Turnover Intention from the Job Satisfaction Scales

When the job satisfaction scales were used to predict turnover intention, three of the scales were statistically significant: internal work motivation, general job satisfaction, and satisfaction with pay, as shown in Table 15. The standardized regression coefficients for general job satisfaction and satisfaction with pay were negative, indicating that higher levels of satisfaction generally and with pay were associated with lower turnover intention. Conversely, internal work motivation was positively associated with turnover intention, indicating that individuals who possessed a large degree of internal work motivation had higher scores on turnover intention. A total of 44.7% of the variance in turnover intention was explained by the job satisfaction scales.

Indirect Effects of Job Characteristics on Turnover Intention

In addition to the direct effects of the job characteristics on the job satisfaction scales (shown in Tables 8 through 14) and the direct effects of the job satisfaction scales on turnover intention (shown in Table 15), indirect effects were computed. These indirect effects were computed between each job characteristic on turnover intention through each job satisfaction scale. The statistical significance of the indirect effects was computed via the Sobol z-test (Sobol, 1982). The Sobol test involves computing the product of the two unstandardized regression coefficients and determining if that product is larger than would be expected if a null hypothesis of no indirect effect were true. However, the product of the unstandardized effects is

Table 15

Prediction of Turnover Intention by the Job Satisfaction Scales

Predictor Variable	β	t	p
Internal Work Motivation	.133	2.769	.006
General Job Satisfaction	-.576	-11.188	<.0005
Satisfaction with Job Security	-.058	-1.290	.198
Satisfaction with Pay	-.160	-3.638	<.0005
Social Job Satisfaction	-.012	-.245	.807
Satisfaction with Supervision	-.073	-1.537	.125
Satisfaction with Job Growth	.001	.010	.992

difficult to interpret because its value depends on the scale of the variables included in either of the effects; thus, the products of the standardized effects are presented here. In total, 63 of these tests (9 job characteristics multiplied by 7 job satisfaction scales) were performed, and 10 were statistically significant. Table 16 contains the standardized value for each of the statistically significant indirect effects of the job characteristics on turnover intention through the job satisfaction scales. As can be seen, each of the 10 statistically significant indirect effects from a job characteristic on turnover intention was through internal work motivation, general satisfaction, or satisfaction with pay. This was expected due to the fact that only these three satisfaction scales had statistically significant direct effects on turnover intention.

Summary of Hypothesis Tests

Sixteen null hypotheses were stated in Chapter Three, organized around two broad research questions.

Research Question 1

The first research question was "Which job characteristic variables contribute to the various dimensions of job satisfaction among software developers?" Nine null hypotheses were stated corresponding to this question, one for each of the nine job characteristics. The first null hypothesis addressed the relationship between organizational commitment to software developer training and the measures of job satisfaction. In the correlational analyses, organizational commitment to training was significantly correlated with all seven job satisfaction scales. Of the seven regression analyses (one for each of the job satisfaction scales) organizational commitment to training was significantly predictive in five (all except internal work motivation and social job satisfaction). Thus, the null hypothesis has been disconfirmed and it can be concluded that

Table 16

Statistically Significant Indirect Effects

Effect	β*β	z	p
Task Sig. → Internal Work Motivation → Turnover Intention	.023	2.051	.040
Feedback → Internal Work Motivation → Turnover Intention	.034	2.306	.021
Training → General Satisfaction → Turnover Intention	-.101	-3.785	<.0005
Number of Devel. → General Satisfaction → Turnover Intention	-.059	-2.261	.024
Skill Variety → General Satisfaction → Turnover Intention	-.072	-2.287	.022
Autonomy → General Satisfaction → Turnover Intention	-.088	-2.400	.016
Feedback → General Satisfaction → Turnover Intention	-.173	-5.036	<.0005
Training → Satisfaction with Pay → Turnover Intention	-.032	-2.657	.008
Number of Devel. → Satisfaction with Pay → Turnover Intention	-.025	-2.301	.021
Feedback → Satisfaction with Pay → Turnover Intention	-.035	-2.487	.013

organizational commitment to training has important relationships with job satisfaction.

The second null hypothesis related to the relationships between the number of developers and the measures of job satisfaction. In the correlational analyses, the number of developers was significantly related to only two of the seven measures of job satisfaction (satisfaction with pay and social job satisfaction). In the regression analyses, the number of developers was significantly predictive of general job satisfaction, satisfaction with pay, social job satisfaction, and satisfaction with supervision. Thus, the null hypothesis was rejected, although it appears that the number of developers was primarily related to satisfaction with pay and social job satisfaction.

The third null hypothesis related to the relationships between the extent to which the respondent had user-contact and the job satisfaction scales. In the correlational analyses, the amount of user-contact was significantly related to all but two of the job satisfaction scales (i.e. all except satisfaction with pay and satisfaction with supervision), although the correlations were modest in magnitude, with the significant correlations ranging from .18 to .26. In the regression analyses, the amount of user-contact was a significant predictor of only satisfaction with job security. Thus, the null hypothesis was rejected, but the size of the relationships between user-contact and job satisfaction is relatively small.

The fourth null hypothesis addressed the relationship between job classification (programmer versus analyst) and the job satisfaction measures. Recall that the method of coding job classification was to assign a value of '0' for programmers and '1' for analysts. Thus, positive correlations between job classification and the job satisfaction scales are indicative of higher levels of satisfaction for analysts. In the correlational analyses, job classification was

103

significantly related to four of the job satisfaction scales, but again these relationships were relatively weak, with the significant correlations ranging from only .11 to .15. In the regression analyses, job classification was only related to satisfaction with job security and satisfaction with supervision, although the correlations between job classification and these measures of satisfaction were not statistically significant. In both cases, the regression coefficient was negative, indicating higher satisfaction in these areas for programmers. Thus, the fourth null hypothesis was rejected, but again these relationships were relatively weak.

The fifth null hypothesis related to the relationships between skill variety and the job satisfaction measures. All seven of the bivariate correlations involving skill variety and the job satisfaction measures were statistically significant. In addition, the magnitude of the correlations tended to be large, ranging from .16 to .63, with four being greater than .40. In the regression analyses, skill variety was significantly predictive of internal work motivation, general job satisfaction, social job satisfaction, and satisfaction with job growth. The fifth null hypothesis was rejected: skill variety is associated with higher job satisfaction.

The sixth null hypothesis was designed to test the relationship between task identity and the measures of job satisfaction. In the correlational analyses, task identity was significantly related to six of the seven job satisfaction scales (all except satisfaction with pay), with the significant correlations ranging from .15 to .47. In the regression analyses, however, task identity was not significantly predictive of any of the job satisfaction scales. One reason for the conflicting findings regarding task identity (i.e. six of the seven bivariate correlations were statistically significant but task identity was not predictive of the job satisfaction scales in the regression analyses) is that task identity tended to be correlated strongly with the other job

104

characteristic variables (see Table 4). That is, while task identity was associated with most of the job satisfaction scales, it was also correlated with the other predictors (the job characteristic scales), reducing its impact in the regression analyses. Nevertheless, the sixth null hypothesis was rejected due to the statistically significant bivariate correlations between task identity and the job satisfaction scales, although it should be noted that task identity is not a central job characteristic in the full model where all of the job characteristics were incorporated as predictors.

The seventh null hypothesis related to the relationships between task significance and the job satisfaction measures. The correlational analyses revealed that task significance was significantly related to six of the seven job satisfaction scales (all except satisfaction with pay). Furthermore, these correlations tended to be large, with the significant correlations ranging from .24 to .47. In the regression analyses, task significance was significantly related to internal work motivation and social job satisfaction. Thus, the seventh null hypothesis was rejected.

The eighth null hypothesis addressed the relationships between autonomy and the measures of job satisfaction. In the correlational analyses, six of the seven correlations were statistically significant (again, all but the correlation with satisfaction with pay). In the regression analyses, autonomy was significantly related to general job satisfaction, satisfaction with supervision, and satisfaction with job growth. Therefore, the eighth null hypothesis was rejected: autonomy was related to most of the measures of job satisfaction.

The ninth null hypothesis addressed the relationships between feedback and the job satisfaction scales. In the bivariate correlation analyses, all seven of the correlations were statistically significant and of substantial size, ranging from .24 to .62. In the regression analyses, feedback was significantly predictive of all seven of the job satisfaction scales. Thus, the ninth null hypothesis was rejected: feedback demonstrated some of the strongest relationships with the job satisfaction scales.

Research Question 2

The second research question was "Which job satisfaction dimensions contribute to turnover intention among software developers?" Seven null hypotheses (10-16) were examined to address this question. The tenth null hypothesis addressed the relationship between internal work motivation and turnover intention. Internal work motivation had a statistically significant bivariate correlation with turnover intention (see Table 7) and was statistically significant as a predictor in the regression analysis (see Table 15). However, the bivariate correlation between internal work motivation and turnover intention was the smallest of any of the job satisfaction scales. In addition, internal work motivation was negatively correlated with turnover intention (indicating that higher internal work motivation corresponded to lower turnover intention), but had a positive regression coefficient in the regression analyses making this relationship somewhat difficult to interpret. Essentially, this means that if only internal work motivation and turnover intention are considered, they are negatively related, but when controlling for the other job satisfaction scales, the relationship was positive. Nevertheless, the tenth null hypothesis was rejected: internal work motivation was related to turnover intention.

The eleventh null hypothesis related to the relationship between general job satisfaction and turnover intention. The bivariate correlation between general job satisfaction and turnover intention was the highest of any of the job satisfaction scales, and general job satisfaction was statistically significant in the regression analysis. Therefore, the eleventh null hypothesis was rejected.

The twelfth null hypothesis addressed the relationship between satisfaction with job security and turnover intention. Although the bivariate correlation between these two variables was statistically significant, satisfaction with job security was not statistically significant in the regression analysis. Nevertheless, the twelfth null hypothesis was rejected due to the statistically significant bivariate correlation.

The thirteenth null hypothesis related to the relationship between satisfaction with pay and turnover intention. Satisfaction with pay was significantly related to turnover intention in both the bivariate correlation analysis and the regression analysis. Therefore, the thirteenth null hypothesis was rejected.

The fourteenth null hypothesis addressed the relationship between social job satisfaction and turnover intention. In the bivariate analysis, these two variables were negatively correlated, but social job satisfaction was not statistically significant in the regression analysis. Nevertheless, the fourteenth null hypothesis was rejected.

The fifteenth null hypothesis related to the relationship between satisfaction with supervision and turnover intention. Again, the bivariate correlation between these two variables was statistically significant, but satisfaction with supervision was not statistically significant as a predictor of turnover intention in the regression analysis. In any case, the fifteenth null hypothesis was rejected.

The sixteenth null hypothesis was designed to test the relationship between satisfaction with job growth and turnover intention. As was the case with satisfaction with job security,

107

social job satisfaction, and satisfaction with supervision, the bivariate correlation was statistically significant, but satisfaction with job growth was not statistically significant in the regression analysis. Nevertheless, the sixteenth null hypothesis was rejected.

In summary, all sixteen of the null hypotheses were rejected due to the fact that some relationship was found between (a) each of the job characteristics and at least one of the job satisfaction scales and (b) each of the job satisfaction scales was related to turnover intention either in the bivariate correlation analyses, or the regression analyses, or both. Nevertheless, substantial variability in terms of the magnitude of these relationships exists, a discussion of which will be presented in Chapter Five.

CHAPTER FIVE: SUMMARY, CONCLUSIONS, AND RECOMMENDATIONS

The final chapter in this study consists of four main subsections. The author begins with a brief summary of the material that has been presented in the previous chapters. Next, an elaborate discussion of the findings from Chapter Four is presented. The study concludes with a discussion of the benefits of these findings for practitioners and some recommendations for future research in this field of study.

Summary

Software developer turnover can have disastrous effects on an organization due to the loss of business process knowledge along with acquired technical skills. Annual rates of turnover in information technology (IT) departments have been estimated at 20% or more (S. Alexander, 1998; S.M. Alexander, 1999; Cone, 1998; Fryer, 1998; Kosseff, 1999; Shurn-Hannah, 2000; Thatcher, Stepna, & Boyle, 2002-03). Estimates of the cost of replacing technology workers range from roughly 1.5 times their annual salaries (Kosseff, 1999) to 2.5 times annual salaries (Longenecker & Scazzero, 2003). The study presented in this dissertation was purposely narrowed to software developers, as opposed to IT employees in general, because developers must understand a user's job in such a thorough manner that the developer can design, code and implement a computerized system to perform some or all of the user's tasks. To be successful, a software developer must have a thorough knowledge of all aspects of the business, as well as the technical skills to make computerization a successful reality. Losing this valuable knowledge and skill can leave a company in a very precarious position and the smaller the company the less backup is available.

The review of the literature showed that the factors leading to turnover intention in this field are poorly understood; therefore, this study was designed to further understand the relationships between job characteristics, job satisfaction, and turnover intention among software developers. The existing body of research has identified a number of factors that impact job satisfaction and turnover intentions among IT employees. This study was designed to explore the dynamic interaction of these factors, through the analysis of data collected via a web survey. The web survey contained questions relating to job characteristics, job satisfaction, turnover intention, and some demographic information. The first four job characteristics are specific to software developers while the last five are from the Job Diagnostic Survey (JDS; Hackman & Oldham, 1985), a general measure to assess job characteristics common to most jobs. The JDS was designed to provide a standardized measure of the key components of an individual's job as they relate to job satisfaction.

Two research questions and sixteen hypotheses were developed to understand which job characteristic variables contribute to the various dimensions of job satisfaction and which job satisfaction dimensions contribute to turnover intention. The model in Figure 1 was developed to depict the interaction between the nine job characteristics and seven job satisfaction variables, and the interaction between the seven job satisfaction variables and turnover intention. The sample for this study was drawn from a global population of IT professionals whose titles are Programmer, Software Engineer, or Programmer Analyst. Survey respondents were recruited via the Internet by posting an invitation to participate in the survey on a series of programming/software development forums and newsgroups. After a two-week period of time, 326 surveys were successfully completed and the survey was removed from the web. Next, a summary of the findings is presented.

Summary of Findings

The summary of the findings of the current study is divided into three areas. First, preliminary findings will be discussed that relate to the reliability of the JDS scales, the correlations among the job characteristics, and the correlations among the job satisfaction scales. Second, the relationships between the job satisfaction scales and turnover intention will be summarized. Third, the relationships between the job characteristics and turnover intention will be addressed.

Preliminary Findings Summary

Analysis of the internal consistency reliability of the scales from the JDS (via Cronbach's α) indicated adequate to high reliability (see Table 3). For the five job characteristic scales, the reliabilities ranged from .76 to .86. For the seven job satisfaction scales, the reliabilities ranged from .74 to .89. Correlational analysis of the nine job characteristic variables (in Table 4) indicated that the highest correlations were among the five job characteristic scales from the JDS, ranging from .31 to .63. The correlations among the job satisfaction scales from the JDS (in Table 5) were all statistically significant and generally high, ranging from .25 to .79. Thus, individuals who were satisfied with some aspects of their job tended to be satisfied with many aspects.

Relationships Between Job Satisfaction and Turnover Intention Summary

In the bivariate correlation analyses (in Table 7), all of the job satisfaction scales were negatively correlated with turnover intention indicating, as was expected, that higher levels of job satisfaction were associated with lower turnover intention. The lowest correlation was between internal work motivation and turnover intention, which is not surprising as internal work motivation is the only job satisfaction scale from the JDS that is not directly tied to a particular aspect of the job, but rather to a general tendency to be motivated to work. The highest correlation was between general job satisfaction and turnover intention, which is also not surprising given that one's overall feelings about a job would be expected to be more strongly related to the intention to quit than feelings about a particular aspect of the job, which could be offset by strong feelings of satisfaction in other areas.

In the regression analysis (in Table 15), general satisfaction was again the strongest predictor of turnover intention. Satisfaction with pay was also statistically significant indicating that, even when controlling for general satisfaction, high satisfaction with pay was enough to reduce intention to quit. Interestingly, internal work motivation was positively related to turnover intention in the regression analyses, whereas it had been negatively related in the bivariate correlational analyses. Thus, when controlling for the various aspects of job satisfaction (in the regression analyses), higher levels of internal work motivation actually increased turnover intention. To understand this ostensibly conflicting result, it is necessary to consider the relationship between internal work motivation and general job satisfaction. There was substantial overlap between internal work motivation and general job satisfaction (which correlated .54 in the bivariate analyses). The part of internal work motivation that was associated with both

112

general job satisfaction and turnover intention was attributed primarily to general job satisfaction in the regression analysis (due to the stronger relationship between general job satisfaction and turnover intention), and the portion of internal work motivation that was left was positively associated with turnover intention. This indicates the value of looking beyond bivariate analyses to multiple regression. At first glance it would appear that higher levels of internal work motivation would produce lower levels of turnover intention, but the negative relationship can be attributed to the overlap between general job satisfaction and internal work motivation. When statistically controlling for the effect of general job satisfaction, higher levels of internal work motivation were actually associated with higher intention to quit.

Relationships Between Job Characteristics and Turnover Intention Summary

The purpose of the indirect effect tests (in Table 16) is to determine if certain job characteristics could be linked to turnover intention through the job satisfaction scales. The results indicated that this was in fact the case, as ten of the indirect effects were statistically significant. All ten of the statistically significant indirect effects were associated with only three of the seven job satisfaction scales: internal work motivation, general job satisfaction, and satisfaction with pay. The largest indirect effect was the effect of autonomy on turnover intention through general job satisfaction: higher levels of autonomy lead to lower levels of turnover intention by increasing general job satisfaction. The next largest indirect effect was the effect of organizational training on turnover intention through general job satisfaction: organizational training decreased turnover intention through an increase in general job satisfaction. The next three highest indirect effects were also between a job characteristic (feedback, skill variety, and number of developers) and turnover intention through general job satisfaction. The statistically

113

significant indirect effects that were transmitted through internal work motivation or satisfaction with pay were relatively small (the highest being -.035), and therefore are of secondary importance.

Elaboration of Hypothesis Testing

Sixteen null hypotheses organized around two broad research questions were stated in Chapter Three.

Research Question 1

The first research question was "Which job characteristic variables contribute to the various dimensions of job satisfaction among software developers?" Nine null hypotheses were stated corresponding to this question, one for each of the nine job characteristics. Table 17 represents a summary of the findings. The first null hypothesis stated the level of organizational commitment to software developer training does not affect the various measures of job satisfaction. The null hypothesis was rejected, which implies that organizational commitment to training has a positive effect on job satisfaction. This supports the findings that lack of professional development opportunities is cited as one of the top three reasons for IT turnover (Hacker, 2003). The importance of training also supports the organizational psychologist Byron Woollen's assertion that IT professionals need to have ample opportunities to refine and develop their technical skills (Fisher, 2000).

The second null hypothesis related to the relationships between the number of developers and the measures of job satisfaction. In the regression analyses, the number of developers was significantly predictive of job satisfaction; thus, the null hypothesis was rejected. This finding may cause a paradox for managers since according to Smits et al. (1993) a striking weakness in

Table 17

Research Question 1 Summary of Job Characteristics and Job Satisfaction Scales

Hypothesis	Job Characteristic	Bivariate	Regression
1	Organizational Training	Yes	Yes
2	Number of Developers	Yes	Yes
3	Work with Users	Yes	Yes
4	Job Classification	Yes	Yes
5	Skill Variety	Yes	Yes
6	Task Identity	Yes	No
7	Task Significance	Yes	Yes
8	Autonomy	Yes	Yes
9	Feedback	Yes	Yes

Note.   "Yes" in the Bivariate column indicates at least one bivariate correlation between this job characteristic and the seven job satisfaction variables was statistically significant at a .01 α level. "Yes" in the Regression column indicates the job characteristic was a statistically significant predictor of at least one job satisfaction scale.

the personality profiles of IT professionals is "interpersonal insensitivity, poor people skills, and a preference for working alone" (p. 114). Smits et al. also cautions that due to their introversion and low interpersonal orientation, IT professionals may present a challenge for managers seeking to socialize them.

The third null hypothesis related to the relationships between the extent to which the respondent had user-contact and the job satisfaction scales. In the correlational analyses, the amount of user-contact was significantly related to all but two of the job satisfaction scales; however, the regression analyses show that the amount of user-contact was a significant predictor only of satisfaction with job security. The null hypothesis was rejected, even though the size of the relationships between user-contact and job satisfaction was relatively small. This supports the assertion that more interaction with users would enhance job satisfaction (Goldstein, 1989).

The fourth null hypothesis addressed the relationship between job classification (programmer versus analyst) and the job satisfaction measures. Job classification was coded with a '0' for programmers and '1' for analysts. The regression coefficient was negative and weak, indicating higher satisfaction for programmers. Thus, the fourth null hypothesis was rejected, since it appears that programmers have a slightly higher degree of satisfaction than analysts. Since the exact job title or job description is hard to define and the line between being primarily a programmer as opposed to predominantly an analyst is blurred, these weak findings are no surprise.

The fifth null hypothesis related to the relationships between skill variety and the job satisfaction measures. All seven of the bivariate correlations involving skill variety and the job

116

satisfaction measures were statistically significant, and the regression analyses showed skill variety to be a significant predictor of four of the seven job satisfaction scales. Thus, the null hypothesis was rejected because skill variety is associated with higher job satisfaction. This finding supports the need for a close alignment of IT and business operations allowing employees to switch between the two areas if they choose (Zetlin, 2001). This also supports the assertion of Smits et al.(1993) that high achievers desire task variety.

The sixth null hypothesis was designed to test the relationship between task identity and the measures of job satisfaction. In the correlational analyses, task identity was significantly related to six of the seven job satisfaction scales, but in the regression analyses, task identity was not significantly predictive of any of the job satisfaction scales due in large part to a strong correlation with the other job characteristic variables. Nevertheless, the sixth null hypothesis was rejected due to the statistically significant bivariate correlations between task identity and the job satisfaction scales. Even though task identity was not a predictor of job satisfaction, its strong correlation to other job characteristic variables and job satisfaction scales makes it worthy of discussion. Role conflict and role ambiguity can undermine job satisfaction and have been identified as contributors to burnout (Goldstein, 1989; Goldstein & Rockart, 1984). Additionally, the organizational psychologist Byron Woollen asserts that managers should explain not only what needs to be done, but also the reason behind it as a method for programmers to understand the strategic importance of their work (Hopkins, 1998; Zetlin, 2001).

The seventh null hypothesis related to the relationships between task significance and the job satisfaction measures. The correlational analyses revealed that task significance was significantly related to six of the seven job satisfaction scales, and the regression analyses shows that task significance is significantly related to internal work motivation and social job satisfaction. Thus, the seventh null hypothesis was rejected, since task significance is related to job satisfaction. This finding supports Lee and Mowday's (1987) assertion that task significance has a positive influence on organizational commitment, and was also positively linked with job satisfaction.

The eighth null hypothesis addressed the relationships between autonomy and the measures of job satisfaction. In the correlational analyses, six of the seven correlations were statistically significant, and in the regression analyses, autonomy was significantly related to general job satisfaction, satisfaction with supervision, and satisfaction with job growth. Thus, the eighth null hypothesis was rejected because autonomy is related to most of the measures of job satisfaction. Amabile (1997) reports that the most creative IT teams boast autonomy and cohesion. This finding is also supported in Igbaria et al. (1991) where they discovered that IT employees have a high need for autonomy and independence.

The ninth null hypothesis addressed the relationships between feedback and the job satisfaction scales. In the bivariate correlation analyses, all seven of the correlations were statistically significant, and in the regression analyses, feedback was significantly predictive of all seven of the job satisfaction scales. Thus, the ninth null hypothesis was rejected because feedback has a very strong relationship with the job satisfaction scales. This finding is of little surprise, since reward, recognition, and feedback appear prominently as strategies for retaining IT talent (Tulgan, 2000; Zemke, 2000; Zetlin, 2001). Additionally, the technology consulting firm Synet Service Corp. organized a forum for clients to share strategies for retaining IT staff

118

(Zemke, 2000). One of the panel's recommendations was to provide consistent, accurate, and timely performance feedback.

Research Question 2

The second research question was "Which job satisfaction dimensions contribute to turnover intention among software developers?" Seven null hypotheses (10-16) were examined to address this question. Table 18 represents a summary of the findings. The tenth null hypothesis addressed the relationship between internal work motivation and turnover intention. Internal work motivation had a statistically significant bivariate correlation with turnover intention and was statistically significant as a predictor in the regression analysis. Internal work motivation was negatively correlated with turnover intention (indicating that higher internal work motivation corresponded to lower turnover intention), but had a positive regression coefficient in the regression analyses making this relationship somewhat difficult to interpret. Regardless, the tenth null hypothesis was rejected since internal work motivation is related to turnover intention.

The eleventh null hypothesis related to the relationship between general job satisfaction and turnover intention. The bivariate correlation between general job satisfaction and turnover intention was the highest of any of the job satisfaction scales, and general job satisfaction was statistically significant in the regression analysis. Therefore, the eleventh null hypothesis was rejected. Even though general job satisfaction is a key component to reducing turnover, Rouse (2001) argues, "Due to the incredible demand for qualified IT professionals, unsolicited job offers are constantly bombarding members of this group." Thus, "Even though there is nothing dissatisfying about their current position, the new offer may be too good to forego" (p. 285). Thatcher et al. (2002-03) concluded that while job market opportunities have a definite impact

119

Table 18

Research Question 2 Summary of Job Satisfaction and Turnover Intention

Hypothesis	Job Satisfaction Scales	Bivariate	Regression
10	Internal Work Motivation	Yes	Yes
11	General Job Satisfaction	Yes	Yes
12	Satisfaction with Job Security	Yes	No
13	Satisfaction with Pay	Yes	Yes
14	Social Job Satisfaction	Yes	No
15	Satisfaction with Supervision	Yes	No
16	Satisfaction with Job Growth	Yes	No

Note. "Yes" in the Bivariate column indicates the correlation between this job satisfaction scale and turnover intention was statistically significant at a .01 α level. "Yes" in the Regression column indicates this job satisfaction scale was a statistically significant predictor of turnover intention.

on the intentions of IT workers to quit, this effect can be offset by organizational programs that provide IT employees with more rewards. In fact, many companies have successfully reduced turnover by creating a work environment that provides IT professionals with the challenging and creative work, professional status and recognition, advancement opportunities, and technology training that are routinely identified as key factors in recruiting and retaining skilled software developers. Many of these job attributes fall under the heading of general job satisfaction.

The twelfth null hypothesis addressed the relationship between satisfaction with job security and turnover intention. Although the bivariate correlation between these two variables was statistically significant, satisfaction with job security was not statistically significant in the regression analysis. Nevertheless, the twelfth null hypothesis was rejected due to the statistically significant bivariate correlation. This finding, at this point in time, is not surprising, especially coming off of a down economy and the crash of many dot.coms that provided all the financial benefits and none of the security. Recent articles suggest that IT professionals are more interested in job security than they had been when jobs were plentiful, although they invariably stress the importance of the workplace environment in attracting and retaining qualified IT staff (McEachern, 2001; Russo, 2002; Walsh, 2001; Zetlin, 2001; Zurier, 2001).

The thirteenth null hypothesis related to the relationship between satisfaction with pay and turnover intention. Satisfaction with pay was significantly related to turnover intention in both the bivariate correlation analysis and the regression analysis. Thus, the thirteenth null hypothesis was rejected, since pay has a direct relationship with turnover intention. The importance of pay is not a surprise and in the 2001 IT Market Compensation Study, which encompassed 198 organizations (roughly 35,000 employees), the number two reason for IT turnover is a significant increase in base pay (Hacker, 2003). Additionally, a national study of IT workers conducted by Minneapolis-based Personnel Decisions International (PDI) reported that salary was second as cited by 74.7% of the sample (Russo, 2002).

The fourteenth null hypothesis addressed the relationship between social job satisfaction and turnover intention. In the bivariate analysis, these two variables were negatively correlated, but social job satisfaction was not statistically significant in the regression analysis. Nevertheless, the fourteenth null hypothesis was rejected since there is a relationship between social job satisfaction and turnover intention. Again, this finding of a weak relationship between social job satisfaction and turnover intention is not surprising given the low need for socialization in introverted people. In fact, Smits et al. (1993) cautions that due to their introversion and low interpersonal orientation, IT professionals may present a challenge for managers seeking to socialize them.

The fifteenth null hypothesis related to the relationship between satisfaction with supervision and turnover intention. Again, the bivariate correlation between these two variables was statistically significant, but satisfaction with supervision was not statistically significant as a predictor of turnover intention in the regression analysis. The null hypothesis was rejected since there is a relationship between satisfaction with supervision and turnover intention. This finding supports Amabile (1997) that positive supervisor support enhances creativity and satisfaction. Additionally, one significant finding of the IRI/Sibson survey is that a bad boss had a particularly powerful impact on the intention to leave (Longenecker & Scazzero, 2003).

The sixteenth and final null hypothesis was designed to test the relationship between satisfaction with job growth and turnover intention. As was the case with satisfaction with job security, social job satisfaction, and satisfaction with supervision, the bivariate correlation was statistically significant, but satisfaction with job growth was not statistically significant in the regression analysis. Nevertheless, the sixteenth null hypothesis was rejected, since there does exist a positive relationship between satisfaction with job growth and turnover intention. Because technology changes so quickly, software developers who perceive their chances for advancement to be stymied will develop insecurity issues and are likely to consider leaving. This lack of job growth issues is ever present in the current literature. McEachern (2001) reports many IT professionals left the financial sector due to lack of respect for their skills and poor opportunities for advancement. Baron et al. (2001) discovered IT workers in non-technology firms are often frustrated by lack of opportunities for professional growth. In a British study of 50 graduates of an organizational graduate training program who had remained with the company for three years, those who perceived opportunities for advancement were satisfied with their jobs, while those who considered themselves "stuck" expressed intentions to leave (Sturges & Guest, 2001).

In summary, all sixteen of the null hypotheses were rejected due to the fact that some relationship was found between each of the job characteristics and at least one of the job satisfaction scales, and each of the job satisfaction scales was related to turnover intention. The prediction of the job satisfaction scales by the job characteristics can be seen in Figure 2. Note that task identity was not statistically significant in the regression and is not shown in the model, and the total paths were reduced from 63 to just 28.

Implications for Practitioners

The results of the study show there are several factors that influence turnover intention among software developers. The job characteristics presented in Figure 1, such as training, autonomy,

Figure 2. Prediction of the job satisfaction scales by the job characteristics

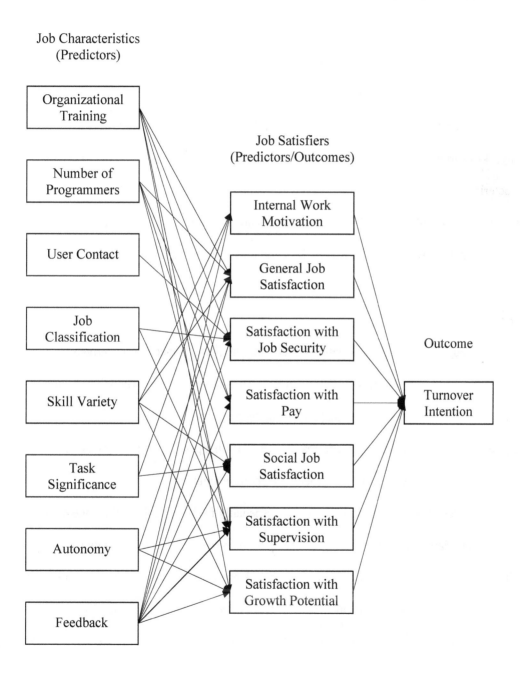

feedback, etc., are all characteristics that can be influenced by management. With the results of this study, management can better understand the unique needs of software developers and design development jobs in such a way to ensure that these needs are met. Five of the nine job characteristics are statistically significant and identified in Table 16, and summarized in Table 19 and Table 20. The five job characteristics listed in descending order of importance based on the number of statistically significant indirect effects are: feedback, training, number of developers, autonomy, skill variety, and task significance. The revised model depicting the indirect effects of job characteristics on turnover intention through job satisfaction is shown in Figure 3. Following, is a description of each of these variables with a discussion concerning programs that can be implemented that directly relate to these variables and hopefully will lead to a reduction in turnover.

Feedback

In this study, feedback is information concerning job performance that is derived from the work itself. Software developers receive positive and negative feedback when they design and code a system. Negative feedback happens when the program code does not compile or does not work as expected. Positive feedback happens when the code is working as expected, is efficient, bug free, on time, meets the requirements, etc.

Software development can be a lonely task, especially for large projects that take a long time to complete. Many times once the requirements of the project are given to the developer who will write the code, the amount of intrinsic feedback can be minimal until there is some part of the code that is up and running and available for testing. Positive peer and supervisory feedback can overcome this lack of intrinsic feedback. Positive communication and

125

Table 19

Frequency of Statistically Significant Indirect Effects

Job Characteristic	Number of Statistically Significant Indirect Effects	Size of the Indirect Effect
Feedback	3	.034, -.173, -.035
Training	2	-.101, -.032
Number of Developers	2	-.059, -.025
Autonomy	1	-.088
Skill Variety	1	-.072
Task Significance	1	.023

Table 20

Summary of Job Characteristics and Turnover Intention

Job Characteristic	Bivariate	Indirect Effects
Organizational Training	Yes	Yes
Skill Variety	Yes	Yes
Task Significance	Yes	Yes
Autonomy	Yes	Yes
Feedback	Yes	Yes
Task Identity	Yes	No
Number of Developers	No	Yes
Work with Users	No	No
Job Classification	No	No

Note. "Yes" in the Bivariate column indicates the correlation between the job characteristic and turnover intention was statistically significant at a .01 α level. "Yes" in the Indirect Effects column indicates at least one statistically significant indirect effect of the job characteristic on turnover intention through a job satisfaction scale.

Figure 3. Indirect effects of job characteristics on turnover intention through job satisfaction

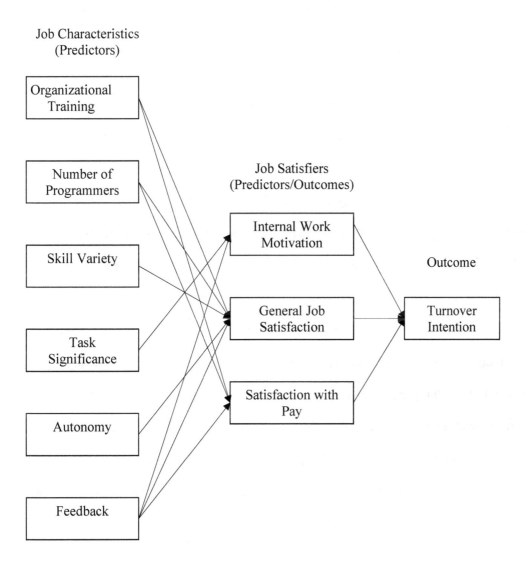

128

acknowledgement of the difficulties in developing software can have a very positive affect, particularly in the early stages of a project when the final product seems out of reach. This is especially true in larger projects and larger groups where a developer can feel like a cog in a big wheel.

Training

Having current skills is a job security issue for software developers because developers with current skills are in high demand. If developers feel that their skills are current due to high-tech projects and formal training, they will be less likely to turn over, since they have an increased sense of security. Technology moves swiftly, and current skills can be outdated skills in a matter of a year or two especially when there is a major shift in technology. Training can be expensive and hard to justify in small organizations, but turnover is much more expensive.

Training is typically cheaper through community colleges or local training companies where travel is not required. Networking through local professional organizations and special interest groups is another inexpensive method for training. Additionally, training one member of the team and having this person train the remaining members is also a viable option and helps the trainer with social and presentation skills, which are sometimes lacking in typically introverted people. Allowing time and expense for training, even if the technology will not be used immediately, gives developers the sense that their skills are current, which increases job security, reduces turnover, and is money well spent.

Number of Programmers

The number of programmers in an organization tends to have a negative effect on the other job characteristics except training. Training is the exception because large organizations typically have more money for training. Since the other job characteristics are negative as the development group size increases it is important to act like a small group even though the number of developers is large. This can be accomplished by forming functional teams that can work as small autonomous units while still maintaining a cohesive larger group. For example, have a code librarian for the entire group of developers to ensure code reuse across the broader group, but still allow for a smaller team to function as an autonomous group. These smaller teams also help to promote a positive social work environment. Another method is to break larger projects into smaller parts and form smaller teams to work on each part. Here again, each team can report its progress to the project manager to help manage the larger project, but the smaller teams will help the developers not feel like just a "small part of a large project," which can greatly reduce the feeling of significance.

Autonomy

In this study autonomy is defined as the degree of freedom or independence in one's job in terms of scheduling and deciding exactly how to carry out the assigned tasks. Software development, especially in a team environment, requires strict adherence to development methodologies, meeting and not exceeding project requirements, following the project design, and many other fairly rigid specifications. This strict adherence to principles and guidelines can reduce the feeling of autonomy and stifle creativity. Many developers have a strong need for autonomy, independence, and creativity; therefore, it is beneficial to structure work as much as possible to meet these needs.

Developers who support and work closely with the end-users tend to work in a less structured and more autonomous environment. This relationship with the users is easy to achieve

130

with an existing system, but more difficult with a new project. To facilitate the creative, autonomous needs of the typical developer, it is advantageous to include the developers in user meetings and allow them the freedom to design the solution, which also educates the developer about business processes. Finally, in many organizations there is a differentiation between analysts and programmers, and in this scenario the autonomy and creativity of the programmer is probably limited due to the analyst having the main user contact. Redesigning the work of programmers to provide them with more autonomy and more interaction with users may enhance job satisfaction.

Skill Variety

Skill variety is the number of diverse skills that a developer can use in various activities. Skill variety can directly relate to training, since without training there may be limited opportunities for expanding one's skills. Skill variety also relates to a feeling of security, since the more skills a developer has, the more job security due to ease of movement. As a developer becomes educated in a particular business process and learns the technology that is used to program these processes, the developer is viewed as the "maintainer" of the system. Relying solely on one developer, as the knowledge base for a particular system, places the organization in a vulnerable position due to limited cross training and coverage.

Software development requires many skills, such as understanding business processes, programming, requirements gathering, data modeling, documentation, testing, etc. Redesigning developers' jobs to allow them to have an opportunity to engage in all these activities will not only create a feeling of security and significance, but also provide redundancy within the organization, which will lead to less disruption in the case of turnover.

Task Significance

Task significance is the extent to which developers perceive that their work has an impact on the world. Developers working on larger projects typically may not see how their piece of the puzzle works as a whole. Management can enhance the perception of their significance by involving the developers in the overall design of the project and allowing them to work with the end-users to receive their feedback. Additionally, involving the developers in user training sessions will allow them to see how important their work is and how it is utilized in the "real world." Involving the developers in user feedback, bug and testing reports, and quality checks will also help solidify the significance of their tasks.

Future Research in Software Developer Turnover

This study focused on turnover in software developers as it relates to job characteristics and subsequent job satisfaction. The intended audience for the survey was developers who worked in an organization as opposed to developers who were self-employed. The invitation letter asking developers to take the survey was intentionally written to exclude self-employed developers. A study of self-employed developers would be beneficial since they do not have management or supervisory issues and may have previously identified and currently adhere to certain job characteristics that make the job satisfying.

A study similar to the present study can focus on contract programmers. A contract programmer works with a client on a contract basis and typically does not become part of the organization as a permanent employee. With this type of relationship, the programmer does not have to deal with issues, such as pay, security, growth potential, etc. Job satisfaction for contract programmers may come more from the type of work and the technical aspects of the task as opposed to organizational issues.

Multiple-choice format makes it quick and easy to fill out and score a survey; however, the respondent's ability to describe job dissatisfaction is severally hampered and can even lead to confusion in the understanding of the survey question. For example, a developer may be happy with the job itself, but dissatisfied with the company's inability to put forth the required effort to successfully market the software product. In this case, the respondent might score general job satisfaction low when in actuality they are happy with the job itself, but dissatisfied with some other aspect that doesn't directly relate to the job. Designing a survey with areas for free-form comments may help uncover some of the real issues behind job dissatisfaction.

In the mid and late 1990s, turnover among software developers was greatly affected by opportunities due to a major shift in technology with the proliferation of the web. Additionally, concerns about software programs being able to handle the four-digit date at the turn of the century presented many lucrative opportunities for software developers. A longitudinal study of this nature would be valuable for determining the effects on job satisfaction and turnover intention as it relates to changes in the economy, major changes in technology and subsequent marketability of skills, effects of outsourcing, and other issues.

A study that takes into consideration the effects of positive and negative corporate culture and how it relates to job satisfaction among software developers would be of great value. Even though many developers work for the love of the development process, and many times are introverted and socially repressed, they still feel the effects of day-to-day corporate life. A study that incorporates some of these values might include such topics as:

1. How morale affects job satisfaction.

2. How various personalities affect job satisfaction, such as introverted as opposed to extroverted.

3. How profitability affects job satisfaction, which can include a company's financial openness and honesty with the employees.

4. Customer retention rate within the organization, which usually points to quality and competitive ability.

5. Overall job stress level.

6. Feeling of value and worth within the organization.

7. Evangelism and leadership from top-levels of management.

Many other variables were captured in the survey, but only utilized as a basis for descriptive statistics. Further analysis is warranted and may lead to a greater understanding of the relationship between these variables and the motivation to leave an organization. Some of these variables that should be considered are:

1. Age

2. Sex

3. Income

4. Education

5. Technology used in the organization, such as current as opposed to old.

6. How the position was obtained, for example, promoted from within the organization.

7. Primary job duties, such as new projects or maintenance programming.

Another recommendation for future research is to further examine the two null hypotheses (sixth and tenth) that show conflicting results between the bivariate correlation and the multiple regression. The sixth null hypothesis was designed to test the relationship between task identity and the measures of job satisfaction. In the correlational analyses, task identity was significantly related to six of the seven job satisfaction scales. In the regression analyses, however, task identity was not significantly predictive of any of the job satisfaction scales. The conflicting findings can be partially explained because task identity tended to be correlated strongly with the other job characteristic variables (see Table 4), which reduces its impact in the regression analyses. Further study of task identity directly related to turnover intention without regards to job satisfiers is warranted.

The tenth null hypothesis addressed the relationship between internal work motivation and turnover intention. Internal work motivation had a statistically significant negative bivariate correlation with turnover intention (see Table 7), but was statistically significant as a positive predictor in the regression analysis (see Table 15). The conflicting findings can be partially explained because the bivariate correlation between internal work motivation and turnover intention was the smallest of any of the job satisfaction scales, and the job satisfaction scales had a high intercorrelation, which implies that they are predicting the same part of turnover intention. Since general job satisfaction easily has the strongest bivariate correlation with turnover intention, the other job satisfaction variables tend to be overshadowed in the regression. A study of internal work motivation relative to turnover intention would be beneficial in further exploring this anomaly.

135

Finally, a study involving IT employees other than software developers, such as network administrators, technical writers, technical support, help-desk, etc. can provide worthwhile data as a basis for comparison with the findings of this study.

List of References

Aiken, L.R. (2000). *Psychological testing and assessment* (10th ed.). Needham Heights, MA: Allyn & Bacon.

Alexander, S. (1998, July 6). Managing IT turnover. *InfoWorld,* 85-86.

Alexander, S.M. (1999, November 1). The tricks for retaining talent. *Crain s Cleveland Business,* T2-T3.

Amabile, T.M. (1997). Motivating creativity in organizations: On doing what you love and loving what you do. *California Management Review, 40,* 39-58.

Amabile, T.M., & Conti, R. (1999). Changes in work environment for creativity during downsizing. *Academy of Management Journal, 42,* 630-640.

Baron, J.N., Hannan, M.T., & Burton, M.D. (2001). Labor pains: Changes in organizational models and employee turnover in young, high-tech firms. *American Journal of Sociology, 106,* 960-1012.

Baroudi, J.J., & Igbaria, M. (1994-95). An examination of gender effects on career success of information systems employees. *Journal of Management Information Systems, 11,* 181-201.

Cohen, A. (1993). Organizational commitment and turnover: A meta-analysis. *Academy of Management Journal, 36,* 1140-1157.

Cone, E. (1998, May 4). Managing that churning sensation. *InformationWeek,* 50-57.

Deakin, M.B. (2002, May 6). Deliver top-drawer training. *Computerworld,* 30-31.

DeMers, A. (2002). Solutions and strategies for it recruitment and retention: A manager's guide. *Public Personnel Management, 31,* 27-40.

Due, R.T. (1992, Winter). The *real* costs of outsourcing. *Information Systems Management,* 78-81.

Ende, J. (1998, August 10). It's 9 a.m., do you know where your tech staff is? *Crain s New York Business,* 18.

Fisher, A. (2000, December 18). Inspiring the burned-out computer programmer [Letter to the editor]. *Fortune,* 334.

Fryer, B. (1998, March 30). IT departments face high staff turnover. *InformationWeek,* 104.

137

Goldstein, D.K. (1989). The effects of task differences on the work satisfaction, job characteristics, and role perceptions of programmer/analysts. *Journal of Management Information Systems, 6,* 41-58.

Goldstein, D.K., & Rockart, J.F. (1984). An examination of work-related correlates of job satisfaction in programmer/analysts. *MIS Quarterly, 8,* 103-462.

Guimares, T., & Igbaria, M. (1992). Determinants of turnover intentions: Comparing IC and IS personnel. *Information Systems Research, 3,* 273-303.

Hacker, C.A. (2003, Spring). Turnover: A silent profit killer. *Information Systems Management,* 14-18.

Hackman, J.R., & Oldham, G.R. (1975). Development of the Job Diagnostic Survey. *Journal of Applied Psychology, 60,* 159-170.

Hackman, J.R., & Oldham, G.R. (1980). *Work Redesign.* Reading, MA: Addison-Wesley.

Herzberg, F. (2003, January). One more time: How do you motivate employees? *Harvard Business Review,* pp. 87-96. (Original article published 1968)

Hopkins, B. (1998, Winter). Productivity shortfall? It's no wonder. *Ivey Business Journal,* pp. 47-51.

Hoyt, J., & Gerloff, E.A. (1999). Organizational environment, changing economic conditions, and the effective supervision of technical personnel: A management challenge. *Journal of High Technology Management Research, 10,* 275-293.

Idaszak, J.R., & Drasgow, F. (1987). A revision of the Job Diagnostic Survey: Elimination of a measurement artifact. *Journal of Applied Psychology, 72,* 69-74.

Igbaria, M., Greenhaus, J.H., & Parasuraman, S. (1991). Career orientations of MIS employees: An empirical analysis. *MIS Quarterly, 15,* 151-169.

Khosrowpour, M., & Subramanian, G.H. (1996). Managing information technologies with outsourcing: An assessment of employee perceptions. *Journal of Applied Business Research, 12*(3), 85-96.

King, R.C., & Sethi, V. (1998). The impact of socialization on the role adjustment of information systems professionals. *Journal of Management Information Systems, 14,* 195-217.

Kochanski, J., & Ledford, G. (2001). 'How to keep me'—Retaining technical professionals. *Research Technology Management, 44*(3), 31-38.

Kosseff, J. (1999, September 6). Info-tech firms increase efforts to keep workers. *Crain s Detroit Business,* p. 21.

Lee, T.W., Mitchell, T.R., Wise, L., & Fireman, S. (1996). An unfolding model of voluntary employee turnover. *Academy of Management Journal, 39,* 5-36.

Lee, T.W., & Mowday, R.T. (1987). Voluntarily leaving an organization: An empirical investigation of Steers and Mowday's model of turnover. *Academy of Management Journal, 30,* 721-743.

Longenecker. C.O., & Scazzero, J.A. (2003, Winter). The turnover and retention of IT managers in rapidly changing organizations. *Information Systems Management,* 59-65.

Lu, C. (1999, June 7). Troubled by turnover? *InfoWorld,* 79-80.

Maidani, E.A. (1991). Comparative study of Herzberg's two-factor theory of job satisfaction among public and private sectors. *Public Personnel Management, 20,* 441-448.

Meares, C.A., & Sargent, J.F. (1999). *The digital work force: Building infotech skills at the speed of innovation.* U.S. Department of Commerce Technology Administration, Office of Technology Policy. Retrieved June 14, 2003, from: http://www.technology.gov/Reports/TechPolicy/digital.pdf.

McEachern, C. (2001, July). The economy may be slowing, but retaining a quality tech department is always key. *Wall Street & Technology,* 43-46.

McGee, M.K. (1996, March 4). Burnout! *InformationWeek,* 34-38.

Moore, J.E. (2000). One road to turnover: An examination of work exhaustion in technology professionals. *MIS Quarterly, 24,* 141-168.

Moses, B. (1997). *Career Intelligence.* Toronto: Stoddart.

Radke, C. (2003, April 18). Bleak outlook for tech workers. *Business Journal Serving Fresno & the Central San Joaquin Valley,* 9-10.

Rouse, P.D. (2001). Voluntary turnover related to information technology professionals: A review of rational and instinctual models. *International Journal of Organizational Analysis, 9,* 281-290.

Russo, P. (2002, July 15). Recruiting, retaining top technology employees. *Food Logistics,* 36-37.

Sanminiatelli, M. (2000, October 23). Study creates tips on hiring and retaining tech employees. *Hudson Valley Business Journal,* 26.

Shurn-Hannah, P. (2000, February). Minority retention strategies alleviate high-tech turnover. *Lightwave,* 127-128.

SmallWaters, Inc. (2001). Analysis of Moment Structures (Version 4.01) [Computer software]. Chicago, IL: SmallWaters, Inc.

Smits, S.J., McLean, E.R., & Tanner, J.R. (1993). Managing high-achieving information systems professionals. *Journal of Management Information Systems, 9,* 103-120.

Sobol, M.E. (1982). Asymptotic intervals for indirect effects in structural equation models. In S. Leinhart (Ed.), *Sociological methodology 1982* (pp. 290-312). San Fransisco: Jossey-Bass.

SPSS, Inc. (2002). Statistical Package for the Social Sciences (Version 11.5) [Computer software]. Chicago, IL: SPSS, Inc.

Sturges, J., & Guest, D. (2001). Don't leave me this way! A qualitative study of influences on the organisational commitment and turnover intentions of graduates early in their career. *British Journal of Guidance & Counseling, 29,* 447-462.

Thatcher, J.B., Stepna, L.P., & Boyle, R.J. (2002-03). Turnover of information technology workers: Examining empirically the influence of attitudes, job characteristics, and external markets. *Journal of Management Information Systems, 19,* 231-261.

Tulgan, B. (2000). *Managing Generation X: How to bring out the best in young talent* (Revised & updated ed.). New York: Norton.

Vandenberg, R.J., & Lance, C.E. (1992). Examining the causal order of job satisfaction and organizational commitment. *Journal of Management, 18,* 153-167.

Walsh, M. (2001, January 1). Techies return to Wall Street. *Crain s New York Business,* 3-4.

Zemke, R. (2000, May). How to hang onto IT talent. *Training,* 42-44.

Zetlin, M. (2001, June 4). Model employers. *Computerworld,* 40-45.

Zurier, S. (2000, April 24). Turning the tables on turnover. *InternetWeek,* 1, 15-18.

APPENDIX A

Human Subjects Review Form

Argosy University-Orange County   IRB#_____ Date Received 2/29/2004

Human Subjects Review - Institutional Review Board

Application for IRB Review of Research Involving the Use of Human Subjects
**Application Status   Exempt___X___(Minimal Risk – HSRC Chair)
                            Expedited _____(Moderate Risk-1 HSRC Member)
                            Regular _____(High Risk - Full HSRC Member Review)

Investigator's Name: _Timothy Lee Doré_____

Social Security Number: On File_____

Address: On File_____

Title of Research Project: The Relationships Between Job Characteristics, Job Satisfaction, and Turnover Intention Among Software Developers____

Name of Chair/Co-Chair: Dr. Judith L. Forbes, Ph.D._____

College and Department: BUS__X____   COBS_____
                                    EDUC_____   OTHER_____

Program and Degree of Study: D.B.A. Information Systems_____

Project Proposed Start Date:_ 1/1/2004_____   Project Proposed Completion Date:_6/30/2004_____

Approval Signatures:_____

Dissertation Committee Chair/Co-Chair/Date_____ /_____

Principal Investigator/Date_____ / 4/1/2004_____

DO NOT PROCEED TO COLLECT DATA PRIOR TO RECEIVING IRB APPROVAL

Important Notice:
- Please complete this form in detail, acquire signatures of the Principal Investigator and the Dissertation Chair, then submit the form to the HSRC Chairperson with attachments relevant to this project (letter of informed consent, questionnaires, test protocol, interview

---

* Category of research must be checked by principal investigator.

questions, observational charts, institutional permission from site where research is to be conducted, parental permission if subject is under 18, completed HSRC form, designated IRB category).

- Do not proceed with any research work with subjects until IRB approval is obtained.

- If any change occurs in the procedure, sample size, research subject, or other element of the project impacts subjects, the HSRC must be notified in writing with the appropriate form (see ancillary forms).

- Please allow 30 days for processing Exempt and Expedited Forms, and 60 days processing for Regular

HSRC contact:_____Date Logged In:_____Date Approved:_____Date Expires:_____

Section A, Exempt Status: Read and complete the following: If you answer yes to any of the following, your research does **NOT** qualify for exempt status and must be checked either Expedited or Regular based on risk/benefit ratio to subjects (If your project does **NOT** qualify for exempt status, **proceed to Section B for Expedited or Regular Status**)

a. Any research with minors or students, except where it only involves the observation of public behavior when investigator(s) do(es) not participate in the activities being observed.　　　Y　　☒

b. Research involving prisoners, fetuses, pregnant women, in vitro fertilization, or any protected groups.　　Y　　☒

c. Research involving intellectually, mentally, or physically challenged members of protected groups.Y　　☒

d. Research involving subject deception of any kind.　　Y　　☒

Note: Exempt status must be approved by HSRC and does NOT mean exempt from use of informed consent.

Please complete Section A below:

1. Study Site and Participants:
    Web based survey completed voluntarily by software developers that frequent various programming forums.

2. Brief but detailed summary of the Project (Attach extra page if needed).

    See attachment entitled "Summary of Project.doc" , which is found in this appendix.

3. Describe the nature of the involvement of human subjects in the project (personal interview, mailed questionnaire, observation, etc. (Attach copy of any instrument, chart, or questionnaire that will be used with subjects).

    This project will utilize an Internet-based survey hosted on the web server at Dolphin Software Inc. An invitation to take the survey will be posted on the sites of Programming/Software Development Forums and Newsgroups. To view the survey please see the attachment entitled "Survey Instrument.doc", which is found in this appendix.

4. Attach a copy of the letter of informed consent.

    See attachment entitled "Survey Instrument.doc" , which is found in this appendix.

5. Describe how confidentiality will be maintained: Be Specific, if using secondary documents, audio/video tapes, etc.

Answering the survey will be anonymous except that the IP addresses will be filtered in order to isolate any duplicates and ensure that no one responds to the survey more than once. It is understood that this procedure is not foolproof. First, it may invalidate some legitimate responses since multiple software developers could be using the same IP address. Alternately, it is possible for one person to respond to the survey multiple times from different IP addresses. To address this possibility the survey will create a cookie that will help to discern whether anyone is attempting to answer the survey twice from the same computer.

6. Describes the exempt category(s) of the project

The purpose of this study is to explore the relationships between job characteristics, job satisfaction, and turnover intention among software developers. This study involves software developers from all over the world developing many different types of software.

7. Signatures and date of review:

Principal Investigator / Date_____ _Jim L. Dore_ ___ / 2/29/2004

Dissertation Committee Chair/Co-Chair / Date_____ / _____

APPENDIX B

Summary of Project Attachment for the HSR Form

Summary of Project

This project will utilize an Internet-based survey hosted on the web server at Dolphin Software Inc. An invitation to take the survey will be posted on the sites of Programming/Software Development Forums and Newsgroups. The study is designed to capture a large pool of programmers, software engineers, and analysts with no inclusion criteria other than job title and job tasks. All respondent information will be acquired through self-reported data. The data derived from the survey will be analyzed and discussed in conjunction with the existing body of related research. The web survey instrument will have two components. The first part is designed to gather basic demographic and employment data, as well as data on some specific characteristics of each respondent's job and organization, and their turnover intention. The second part contains questions from the Job Diagnostic Survey (JDS; Oldham & Hackman, 1975).

The JDS (Oldham & Hackman, 1975) was designed to provide a standardized measure of the key components of an individual's job as they related to job satisfaction. A revised version of the scale was presented by Idaszak and Drasgow (1987) in which the revision of previously reverse-scored items resulted in scales with better psychometric properties. The revised version of the scale will be employed in the present study. The JDS consists of five job characteristic scales (skill variety—3 items, task identity—3 items, task significance—3 items, autonomy—3 items, and feedback—3 items) and seven job satisfaction scales (internal work motivation—6 items, general job satisfaction—5items, satisfaction with job security—2 items, satisfaction with pay—2 items, social job satisfaction—3 items, satisfaction with supervision—3 items, and

147

satisfaction with growth potential—4 items). The particular items composing each scale will be provided.

Respondents will be asked whether they would like a copy of the survey results upon completion. Those who do so will be asked for an e-mail address. All respondents will be assured of complete anonymity.

Both descriptive and inferential statistical methods will be employed. Descriptive statistics (percentages, means, and standard deviations) will be used to characterize the sample in terms of demographic characteristics, job characteristics, job satisfaction, and turnover intention. Correlations will be presented between all of the study variables prior to the main set of inferential analyses. The primary inferential technique to be employed will be path analysis. Path analysis is an extension of multiple regression analysis in which selected variables can be employed as both predictor variables and outcome variables. In the present study, it is the job satisfaction variables that will take this dual role. The various job satisfaction variables will be modeled as outcomes of the job characteristic variables and as predictors of turnover intention.

References

Hackman, J.R., & Oldham, G. R. (1975). Development of the Job Diagnostic Survey. *Journal of Applied Psychology, 60,* 159-170.

Idaszak, J.R., & Drasgow, F. (1987). A revision of the Job Diagnostic Survey: Elimination of a measurement artifact. *Journal of Applied Psychology, 72,* 69-74.

APPENDIX C

Web Survey

Part 1

Your e-mail address will remain confidential and is only needed to send you a copy of the results, as well as, enter you in a drawing for one of four $50 gift certificates to Amazon.com.

Optional e-mail address: [INPUT BOX]

1. Age: [INPUT BOX]

2. Gender: ( ) Male   ( ) Female

3. Years as a software developer/analyst: [INPUT BOX]

4. Years at current organization: [INPUT BOX]

5. Years in current position: [INPUT BOX]

6. Number of software developers/analysts in current organization: [INPUT BOX]

7. Salary:

    ( ) Below $30,000
    ( ) $30,000 - $40,000
    ( ) $40,001 – $50,000
    ( ) $50,001 – $60,000
    ( ) $60,001 - $70,000
    ( ) $70,001 - $80,000
    ( ) Above $80,000

8. Education:

( ) High school diploma
( ) Some college
( ) Completed a computer-related bachelor's degree
( ) Completed a bachelor's degree in another discipline
( ) Completed a computer-related graduate degree
( ) Completed a graduate degree in another discipline

9. Primary job title:

( ) Programmer
( ) Software engineer
( ) Programmer/Analyst
( ) Systems analyst
( ) Other [INPUT BOX]

10. How often do you work directly with the users of the software you develop?

( ) Never
( ) Rarely
( ) Sometimes
( ) Frequently
( ) Always

11. Relative to today s technology, the technology you develop is:

( ) A clay tablet
( ) Pencil and paper
( ) Barely electronic
( ) Fairly current
( ) State-of-the-art

12. Your work preference is to:

( ) Just write code
( ) Some design/analysis
( ) Moderate design/analysis
( ) Heavy design/analysis
( ) Virtually all phases of the software development life cycle

13. Which of these two job descriptions describes your job best?

( ) Write code, test, debug, documentation
( ) Problem analysis, design solutions, write a little code, work with users

14. To what extent do you understand the business impact of your daily work?

( ) I'm clueless
( ) A little
( ) Somewhat
( ) Quite a bit
( ) Completely

15. What is your visibility within your organization?

( ) Anonymous
( ) Low visibility
( ) Moderate visibility
( ) High visibility
( ) Everyone knows me

16. How committed is your organization to providing software development training?

( ) No money
( ) A little money
( ) A reasonable amount of money
( ) A lot of money
( ) Unlimited money

17. In your organization the development process is:

( ) Chaotic
( ) Semi-structured
( ) Methodology defined
( ) Formal System/Software Development Life Cycle (SDLC)
( ) Very formal

152

18. How did you obtain your current position?

( ) Promoted/transferred from a non-programming position within current organization
( ) Promoted/transferred from a programming position within current organization
( ) Hired through a headhunter
( ) Recruited by the organization
( ) Applied for an advertised position
( ) Other [INPUT BOX]

19. What is your primary duty?

( ) Developing new systems
( ) Maintaining/enhancing existing systems
( ) An equal mix of new and existing systems
( ) Other [INPUT BOX]

20. How would you characterize your intentions to seek a new job with a different organization?

( ) I'm ready to go
( ) I could be lured away easily
( ) I may leave but am not desperate to go
( ) I am not presently considering leaving this organization
( ) I'd have to be dragged out of here

21. How long in years do you currently plan to continue working with your current organization?

( ) [INPUT BOX] Years
( ) Until retirement (in about [INPUT BOX] years)

Part 2, Section 1

This part of the questionnaire asks you to describe your job, as *objectively* as you can. Please do not use this part of the questionnaire to show how much you like or dislike your job. Questions about that will come later. Instead, try to make your descriptions as accurate and as objective as you possibly can.

1. To what extent does your job require you to *work closely with other people* (either "clients," or people in related jobs in your own organization)?

1	2	3	4	5	6	7
( )	( )	( )	( )	( )	( )	( )

Very little: dealing with other people is not at all necessary in doing my job

Moderately: some dealing with others is necessary

Very much: dealing with other people is an absolutely essential and crucial part of my job

2. How much autonomy is in your job? That is, to what extent does your job permit you to decide *on your own* how to go about doing the work?

1	2	3	4	5	6	7
( )	( )	( )	( )	( )	( )	( )

Very little: the job gives me almost no personal "say" in how and when the work is done

Moderate autonomy: many things are standardized and not under my control, but I can make some decisions about the work

Very much: the job gives me almost complete responsibility for deciding how and when the work is done

3. To what extent does your job involve doing a *whole and identifiable piece of work*? That is, is the job a complete piece of work that has an obvious beginning and end? Or is it only a small *part* of the overall piece of work, which is finished by other people or by automatic machines?

```
          1      2      3      4      5      6      7
         ( )    ( )    ( )    ( )    ( )    ( )    ( )
```

My job is only a tiny part of the overall piece of work; the results of my activities cannot be seen in the final product or service	My job is a moderate-sized "chunk" of the overall piece of work; my own contribution can be seen in the final outcome	My job involves doing the whole piece of work, from start to finish; the results of my activities are easily seen in the final product or service

4. How much *variety* is in your job? That is, to what extent does the job require you to do many different things at work, using a variety of your skills and talents?

```
          1      2      3      4      5      6      7
         ( )    ( )    ( )    ( )    ( )    ( )    ( )
```

Very little: the job requires me to do the same routine things over and over again	Moderate variety	Very much: the job requires me to do many different things, using a number of different skills and talents

5. In general, how *significant or important* is your job? That is, are the results of your work likely to significantly affect the lives or well-being of other people?

```
          1      2      3      4      5      6      7
         ( )    ( )    ( )    ( )    ( )    ( )    ( )
```

Not very significant: the outcomes of my work are *not* likely to have important effects on other people	Moderately significant	Highly significant: the outcomes of my work can affect other people in very important ways

6. To what extent do *managers or co-workers* let you know how well you are doing on your job?

1	2	3	4	5	6	7
( )	( )	( )	( )	( )	( )	( )

Very little: people almost never let me know how well I am doing

Moderately: sometimes people may give me "feedback"; other times they may not

Very much: managers or co-workers provide me with almost constant "feedback" about how well I am doing

7. To what extent does doing the job itself provide you with information about your work performance? That is, does the actual work itself provide clues about how well you are doing—aside from any "feedback" co-workers or supervisors may provide?

1	2	3	4	5	6	7
( )	( )	( )	( )	( )	( )	( )

Very little: the job itself is set up so I could work forever without finding out how well I am doing

Moderately: sometimes doing the job provides "feedback" to me; sometimes it does not

Very much: the job is set up so that I get almost constant "feedback" as I work about how well I am doing

156

Part 2, Section 2

Listed below are a number of statements, which could be used to describe a job. You are to indicate whether each statement is an accurate or an inaccurate description of your job. Once again, please try to be as objective as you can in deciding how accurately each statement describes your job—regardless of whether you like or dislike your job.

1. The job requires me to use a number of complex or high-level skills.

1	2	3	4	5	6	7
( )	( )	( )	( )	( )	( )	( )
Very Inaccurate	Mostly Inaccurate	Slightly Inaccurate	Uncertain	Slightly Accurate	Mostly Accurate	Very Accurate

2. The job requires a lot of cooperative work with other people.

1	2	3	4	5	6	7
( )	( )	( )	( )	( )	( )	( )
Very Inaccurate	Mostly Inaccurate	Slightly Inaccurate	Uncertain	Slightly Accurate	Mostly Accurate	Very Accurate

3. The job is arranged so that I can do an entire piece of work from beginning to end.

1	2	3	4	5	6	7
( )	( )	( )	( )	( )	( )	( )
Very Inaccurate	Mostly Inaccurate	Slightly Inaccurate	Uncertain	Slightly Accurate	Mostly Accurate	Very Accurate

4. Just doing the work required by the job provides many chances for me to figure out how well I am doing.

1	2	3	4	5	6	7
( )	( )	( )	( )	( )	( )	( )
Very Inaccurate	Mostly Inaccurate	Slightly Inaccurate	Uncertain	Slightly Accurate	Mostly Accurate	Very Accurate

5. The job is quite complex and requires that I engage in a number of different tasks.

1	2	3	4	5	6	7
( )	( )	( )	( )	( )	( )	( )
Very Inaccurate	Mostly Inaccurate	Slightly Inaccurate	Uncertain	Slightly Accurate	Mostly Accurate	Very Accurate

6. The job can be done adequately by a person working alone—without talking or checking with other people.

1	2	3	4	5	6	7
( )	( )	( )	( )	( )	( )	( )
Very Inaccurate	Mostly Inaccurate	Slightly Inaccurate	Uncertain	Slightly Accurate	Mostly Accurate	Very Accurate

7. The supervisors and co-workers on this job almost always give me "feedback" about how well I am doing in my work.

1	2	3	4	5	6	7
( )	( )	( )	( )	( )	( )	( )
Very Inaccurate	Mostly Inaccurate	Slightly Inaccurate	Uncertain	Slightly Accurate	Mostly Accurate	Very Accurate

8. The job is one where a lot of other people can be affected by how well the work gets done.

1	2	3	4	5	6	7
( )	( )	( )	( )	( )	( )	( )
Very Inaccurate	Mostly Inaccurate	Slightly Inaccurate	Uncertain	Slightly Accurate	Mostly Accurate	Very Accurate

9. The job gives me a chance to use my personal initiative or judgment in carrying out the work.

1	2	3	4	5	6	7
( )	( )	( )	( )	( )	( )	( )
Very Inaccurate	Mostly Inaccurate	Slightly Inaccurate	Uncertain	Slightly Accurate	Mostly Accurate	Very Accurate

10. Supervisors often let me know how well they think I am performing the job.

1	2	3	4	5	6	7
( )	( )	( )	( )	( )	( )	( )
Very Inaccurate	Mostly Inaccurate	Slightly Inaccurate	Uncertain	Slightly Accurate	Mostly Accurate	Very Accurate

11. The job provides me the chance to completely finish the pieces of work I begin.

1	2	3	4	5	6	7
( )	( )	( )	( )	( )	( )	( )
Very Inaccurate	Mostly Inaccurate	Slightly Inaccurate	Uncertain	Slightly Accurate	Mostly Accurate	Very Accurate

12. After I finish a job, I know whether I performed well.

1	2	3	4	5	6	7
( )	( )	( )	( )	( )	( )	( )
Very Inaccurate	Mostly Inaccurate	Slightly Inaccurate	Uncertain	Slightly Accurate	Mostly Accurate	Very Accurate

13. The job gives me considerable opportunity for independence and freedom in how I do the work.

1	2	3	4	5	6	7
( )	( )	( )	( )	( )	( )	( )
Very Inaccurate	Mostly Inaccurate	Slightly Inaccurate	Uncertain	Slightly Accurate	Mostly Accurate	Very Accurate

14. The job itself is very significant or important in the broader scheme of things.

1	2	3	4	5	6	7
( )	( )	( )	( )	( )	( )	( )
Very Inaccurate	Mostly Inaccurate	Slightly Inaccurate	Uncertain	Slightly Accurate	Mostly Accurate	Very Accurate

Part 2, Section 3

Now please indicate how *you personally feel about your job*. Each of the statements below is something that a person might say about his or her job. You are to indicate your own personal *feelings* about your job by marking how much you agree with each of the statements.

1. My opinion of myself goes up when I do this job well.

1	2	3	4	5	6	7
( )	( )	( )	( )	( )	( )	( )
Disagree Strongly	Disagree	Disagree Slightly	Neutral	Agree Slightly	Agree	Agree Strongly

2. Generally speaking, I am very satisfied with this job.

1	2	3	4	5	6	7
( )	( )	( )	( )	( )	( )	( )
Disagree Strongly	Disagree	Disagree Slightly	Neutral	Agree Slightly	Agree	Agree Strongly

3. I feel a great sense of personal satisfaction when I do this job well.

1	2	3	4	5	6	7
( )	( )	( )	( )	( )	( )	( )
Disagree Strongly	Disagree	Disagree Slightly	Neutral	Agree Slightly	Agree	Agree Strongly

4. I rarely think of quitting this job.

1	2	3	4	5	6	7
( )	( )	( )	( )	( )	( )	( )
Disagree Strongly	Disagree	Disagree Slightly	Neutral	Agree Slightly	Agree	Agree Strongly

5. I feel bad or unhappy when I discover that I have performed poorly on this job.

1	2	3	4	5	6	7
( )	( )	( )	( )	( )	( )	( )
Disagree Strongly	Disagree	Disagree Slightly	Neutral	Agree Slightly	Agree	Agree Strongly

6. I am generally satisfied with the kind of work I do in this job.

1	2	3	4	5	6	7
( )	( )	( )	( )	( )	( )	( )
Disagree Strongly	Disagree	Disagree Slightly	Neutral	Agree Slightly	Agree	Agree Strongly

7. My own feelings generally are affected by how well I do on this job.

1	2	3	4	5	6	7
( )	( )	( )	( )	( )	( )	( )
Disagree Strongly	Disagree	Disagree Slightly	Neutral	Agree Slightly	Agree	Agree Strongly

Part 2, Section 4

Now please indicate how satisfied you are with each aspect of your job listed below.

1. The amount of job security I have.

1	2	3	4	5	6	7
( )	( )	( )	( )	( )	( )	( )
Extremely Dissatisfied	Dissatisfied	Slightly Dissatisfied	Neutral	Slightly Satisfied	Satisfied	Extremely Satisfied

2. The amount of pay and fringe benefits I receive.

1	2	3	4	5	6	7
( )	( )	( )	( )	( )	( )	( )
Extremely Dissatisfied	Dissatisfied	Slightly Dissatisfied	Neutral	Slightly Satisfied	Satisfied	Extremely Satisfied

3. The amount of personal growth and development I get in doing my job.

1	2	3	4	5	6	7
( )	( )	( )	( )	( )	( )	( )
Extremely Dissatisfied	Dissatisfied	Slightly Dissatisfied	Neutral	Slightly Satisfied	Satisfied	Extremely Satisfied

4. The people I talk to and work with on my job.

1	2	3	4	5	6	7
( )	( )	( )	( )	( )	( )	( )
Extremely Dissatisfied	Dissatisfied	Slightly Dissatisfied	Neutral	Slightly Satisfied	Satisfied	Extremely Satisfied

5. The degree of respect and fair treatment I receive from my boss.

1	2	3	4	5	6	7
( )	( )	( )	( )	( )	( )	( )
Extremely Dissatisfied	Dissatisfied	Slightly Dissatisfied	Neutral	Slightly Satisfied	Satisfied	Extremely Satisfied

6. The feeling of worthwhile accomplishment I get from doing this job.

1	2	3	4	5	6	7
( )	( )	( )	( )	( )	( )	( )
Extremely Dissatisfied	Dissatisfied	Slightly Dissatisfied	Neutral	Slightly Satisfied	Satisfied	Extremely Satisfied

7. The chance to get to know other people while on the job.

1	2	3	4	5	6	7
( )	( )	( )	( )	( )	( )	( )
Extremely Dissatisfied	Dissatisfied	Slightly Dissatisfied	Neutral	Slightly Satisfied	Satisfied	Extremely Satisfied

8. The amount of support and guidance I receive from my supervisor.

1	2	3	4	5	6	7
( )	( )	( )	( )	( )	( )	( )
Extremely Dissatisfied	Dissatisfied	Slightly Dissatisfied	Neutral	Slightly Satisfied	Satisfied	Extremely Satisfied

9. The degree to which I am fairly paid for what I contribute to this organization.

1	2	3	4	5	6	7
( )	( )	( )	( )	( )	( )	( )
Extremely Dissatisfied	Dissatisfied	Slightly Dissatisfied	Neutral	Slightly Satisfied	Satisfied	Extremely Satisfied

10. The amount of independent thought and action I can exercise in my job.

1	2	3	4	5	6	7
( )	( )	( )	( )	( )	( )	( )
Extremely Dissatisfied	Dissatisfied	Slightly Dissatisfied	Neutral	Slightly Satisfied	Satisfied	Extremely Satisfied

11. How secure things look for me in the future of this organization.

1	2	3	4	5	6	7
( )	( )	( )	( )	( )	( )	( )
Extremely Dissatisfied	Dissatisfied	Slightly Dissatisfied	Neutral	Slightly Satisfied	Satisfied	Extremely Satisfied

12. The chance to help other people while at work.

1	2	3	4	5	6	7
( )	( )	( )	( )	( )	( )	( )
Extremely Dissatisfied	Dissatisfied	Slightly Dissatisfied	Neutral	Slightly Satisfied	Satisfied	Extremely Satisfied

13. The amount of challenge in my job.

1	2	3	4	5	6	7
( )	( )	( )	( )	( )	( )	( )
Extremely Dissatisfied	Dissatisfied	Slightly Dissatisfied	Neutral	Slightly Satisfied	Satisfied	Extremely Satisfied

14. The overall quality of the supervision I receive in my work.

1	2	3	4	5	6	7
( )	( )	( )	( )	( )	( )	( )
Extremely Dissatisfied	Dissatisfied	Slightly Dissatisfied	Neutral	Slightly Satisfied	Satisfied	Extremely Satisfied

Part 2, Section 5

Now please think of the other people in your organization who hold the same job you do. If no one has exactly the same job as you, think of the job, which is most similar to yours. Think about how accurately each of the statements describes the feelings of those people about the job. It is quite alright if your answers here are different from when you described your *own* reactions to the job. Often different people feel quite differently about the same job.

1. Most people on this job feel a great sense of personal satisfaction when they do the job well.

1	2	3	4	5	6	7
( )	( )	( )	( )	( )	( )	( )
Disagree Strongly	Disagree	Disagree Slightly	Neutral	Agree Slightly	Agree	Agree Strongly

2. Most people on this job are very satisfied with the job.

1	2	3	4	5	6	7
( )	( )	( )	( )	( )	( )	( )
Disagree Strongly	Disagree	Disagree Slightly	Neutral	Agree Slightly	Agree	Agree Strongly

3. People on this job often think of quitting.

1	2	3	4	5	6	7
( )	( )	( )	( )	( )	( )	( )
Disagree Strongly	Disagree	Disagree Slightly	Neutral	Agree Slightly	Agree	Agree Strongly

4. Most people on this job feel bad or unhappy when they find that they have performed the work poorly.

1	2	3	4	5	6	7
( )	( )	( )	( )	( )	( )	( )
Disagree Strongly	Disagree	Disagree Slightly	Neutral	Agree Slightly	Agree	Agree Strongly

APPENDIX D

Letter of Informed Consent

Thank you for voluntarily taking this survey.

Please be as honest as possible and answer all questions to the best of your knowledge. You should be able to complete the survey in about 10 minutes. Once the study is completed, a summary of the results will be made available to all respondents that have supplied their e-mail address.

Your participation in this survey is entirely voluntary and anonymous, except your IP Address will be recorded and a cookie will be created to help ensure no duplicate surveys. By completing this survey you are giving your consent to be involved in the research. If at any point you decide that you do not want to complete the survey, please click the **Cancel** button and your responses will not be recorded. While taking the survey, please feel free to ask any questions you may have by clicking the **E-mail Researcher** button. Your questions will be answered promptly.

Thank you for your cooperation and the time that you have put into taking this survey. Your time is valuable and I truly appreciate your help.

Thank you,

Tim Doré

APPENDIX E

Letter Inviting Developers to Take the Survey

Subject: Software Developer earning his Doctorate needs help

I have been a Software Developer for 25 years mostly PC based for the last 20. I have been earning my Doctorate for the past 4 years and am now in the dissertation phase of my studies. The theme of my dissertation is the relationships between job characteristics, job satisfaction and turnover intention among Software Developers. I have developed a model that shows the paths from job characteristics such as autonomy or task significance to job satisfiers such as internal work motivation or satisfaction with pay, and ending with the Developer's turnover intention (quitting their job in the near future). Survey data will drive the model and will hopefully serve as a basis for structuring programs and policies to promote the retention of Software Developers.

I am intentionally limiting my study to developers that are "part of an organization". In other words, I am limiting the study to developers that are not self-employed nor contract programmers. If you're a Software Developer that works for an organization I would truly appreciate it if you would take a few minutes out of your busy schedule and take my survey at **http://www.dolphinmsds.com/progsurvey**

Your e-mail address is optional but if you leave it I will send you a copy of my dissertation in the next 90 days. I will also have a drawing for 4 Amazon $50 gift certificates for survey participants. The survey results will be very helpful for future developers and for management to understand the nature of developers. Feel free to ask your developer friends, and I sincerely thank you for your help.

Tim Doré

www.ingramcontent.com/pod-product-compliance
Lightning Source LLC
Chambersburg PA
CBHW060133060326
40690CB00018B/3855